ONE NIGHT STANDS

CHRIS HARDERS

CHRIS HARDERS

ISBN: 0692395385
ISBN-13: 978-0692395387

YOUR FREE LIMITED TIME GIFT!

As a way of saying thank you for your purchase, I'm offering a limited time only free video report on how to close the girl. This is secret footage I took of when I was out at the bar with a girl I had just met. You will see not only the whole dialogue building up to the date, but also the steps I take to get her naked and moaning when we are back at her place.

To check out the video, go to getthegirltonight.com/one-night-stands.

Warning: The video is graphic. You will see breasts and hear her orgasming (a lot). I wanted you to get all access. For that same reason, the video can be taken down at anytime if the girl finds out about it.

CHRIS HARDERS

CONTENTS

CHRIS HARDERS

ABOUT THIS BOOK

I started out like most guys who get involved in "the game." I was inexperienced with women. I was a virgin until 23. I used to imagine the day I would be a player. I knew a life full of beautiful women was possible because I had seen guys with the hot women I wanted some day. I thought, *"If they can do it, I can do it."*

I was confident I would one day be a player, but I did not know where to begin. There was so much bad advice about how to meet women... I had friends telling me things would "just happen," but these friends were dating girls I did not consider attractive. Plus, the girls my friends were dating had made all the first moves. My family told me to "just be myself." Clearly, that was not working for me. The girls I had gone on dates with never gave reasons why they would not see me for a second date. The internet was littered with articles that were even weirder, telling me to do magic tricks or be a jerk to girls. There were the guys I met in bars who would say I needed to "take more shots."

I now know all of the advice I was hearing was terrible. The advice was the OPPOSITE of good game. I solved my woman problem by meeting a group of self-proclaimed players who offered me the chance to live with them. These new mentors told me that I would become amazing with meeting women by living with them and learning by observation. I was doubtful of their claims but decided to give these guys a chance. Two weeks after moving in with them, I lost my virginity. Within three months, I had slept with 13 women. Fast-forward three years and I have slept with over 100 women. I do not tell you these numbers to brag. I tell you so you know I am not full of shit. The system works. I learned the system from the advice of these players combined with my personal innovations.

The players were right. The best way to learn to have One Night Stands is through personal experience and reference experience. While I have heard guys adopt the Nike philosophy of ***Just Do It*** to learn the game, reference experience in the form of stories and observation is an accelerator to game growth because you can learn how things actually go down and take similar actions in your own life and you will internalize a stronger belief in how everything works.

This book is a culmination of some of my best lay reports. These are all true stories. Read them and enjoy them. The knowledge you are about to learn will improve your game.

One Night Stands are not that hard… as long as you have an idea of what to do…

MELLY

Max and I see a high energy crazy two set. Max opens, and I come in seconds later. They are from Australia.... Break in rapport here I go... I say, "Oh really! I just saw a documentary on Australia: Crocodile Dundee."

The girls laugh.

Then, I ask some logistical questions that they answer. I find out that the two girls are sisters. They are out celebrating their oldest sister's wedding, which is the next day. Melly is the youngest sister, and the other girl Alice is the middle sister. The entire wedding party is out at the club with them that night, including the bride (their sister), the groom, and a few other friends.

Melly has such high energy and is dancing around all crazy and fast. She starts dancing with me. And by "dancing," I don't mean Salsa or grinding or a dance with rhythm; I mean, it's ballroom dancing meets WWE on crack. She's chest bumping me and jumping into my arms. She's having me twirl her around. She's wrapping her legs around me while I spin her in circles. How I do not drop her is beyond my comprehension.

The girls want us to go over and meet the rest of the

wedding party. I talk to the bride and congratulate her on getting married and say that I have a lot of friends around town, so if they need anything while they are in town, they should not hesitate to let me know. She is very thankful.

At this point, no other guys are hitting on Melly, but there are a ton of creepers nearby. Melly tells me that I am the most fun person she's met because no one else will twirl her, and I know that's a good sign.

I come up with a reason for Melly and I to disappear from the sight of the rest of the group for a second. We are sitting on a giant bed. I know this is where I am supposed to kiss her, but I am nervous for the right signal that it's okay to do, so we're talking while I'm trying to think of how my lips are supposed to end up on her lips without things being creepy or weird. She tells me stuff about the wedding and her family. Then blurts out that she is going to have sex tonight; she pauses, realizing what she just said, covers her mouth and says, "I mean, I'm not going to have sex tonight."

I smile. I couldn't have asked for a better invitation to kiss her. We start making out. I forgot to ask where the girls were staying earlier. I ask now. I find out that Melly and her sister don't have a place to stay tonight, so logistics are getting even better. At this point, I know I am good with Melly. I should make friends with the family, so they are okay with me being with Melly.

I let Melly be a crazy fun social girl, running around and dancing while I talk more with the sister and fiancé, asking what their plans are after the wedding and where they are going to go for their honeymoon. Melly comes into the conversation and says she wants to buy me a drink. We head to the bar. We get separated because of the crowd, and a creepy PUA makes a beeline for Melly. I already know the other PUA has no shot with her and decide to let him blow himself out, rather than come into the conversation. I go back over to the family, figuring Melly will find me eventually.

She finds me and drags me back by the hand back to the bar, saying how weird the other PUA is and how he is trying to follow her and make out and was being really needy.

She orders a drink for each of us. They can't take her card because it doesn't have her name on it, so I think *"Fuck it"* and pay $40 for 2 Red Bull vodkas. I figure that is breaking a technical rule in game buy paying for the drink, but I also figure rules are made to be broken in the name of pussy, especially when I'm not doing this as a DHV. I'm paying to not break state by seeming like a cheap ass and by forcing her to have to go ask for money from her relatives.

We hang out and talk at the bar a few more minutes. Then, we go back to the family. I continue to build comfort with the family and occasionally dance with Melly. Melly's older sister tells me, I seem like a great guy. She asks what me and Max's intentions are with Melly and Alice (Max has been gaming Alice this whole time).

I say, "I am just having fun."

The older sister asks what I have in mind.

I say, "Nothing, we'll see where the night takes us."

The oldest sister says, she trusts her sisters, and Max and I seem like good guys. I keep talking to the old sister. Meanwhile, Melly keeps telling me how we'll wait til the oldest sister and fiancé leave, then go back to my place. I'm happy she's doing the thinking for me.

Finally, at 4:30am Surrender closes, and we leave. Melly is hilarious. She goes to use the bathroom on the way out but does not come out for 20 minutes. Alice comes up to me and asks what is going on. I say, "I'm not sure."

Alice goes in and drags Melly out of the bathroom. Melly had a conversation with one of the janitors and felt that it was unfair the janitor had to mop all of the bathrooms, so Melly was helping her... Alice grab Melly by the elbow and leads her toward the exit of the club before letting go.

Then, we leave the club. Alice and Melly decide we all need to walk with the older sister back to the hotel... At Bellagio!! I start laughing because I know we're going to do it, and I know Max is pissed. He starts trying to convince them we need a taxi. With this group, it's a lost cause. They don't want a taxi. They want to walk!

So, then comes the journey home... The journey consists of me giving Melly piggy back rides and racing each other, brief making out, and twirling.

Melly asks me if she can sleep at my place. I say, "Yes."

When we are one hotel away from Bellagio, the oldest sister tells Melly and Alice they do not need to keep walking with her. They hug goodbye, and the older sister gives a look of warning to Max and I. Max, Alice, Melly, and I hop in a cab and get to our place.

At our place, we go out to the pool. Melly's feet are filthy from walking bare foot from the club toward the Bellagio since her heels were hurting. She says she needs her feet washed, so I take her into the main bathroom, have her sit on the counter, and I wash her feet in the sink. I dry them then bring her into my room,.

Once we're in the room, she knows EXACTLY what to do (which is great, since I don't!). We make out. I start to take off my shirt. She says she needs to go to the bathroom. I debate how undressed I should get while she's gone. She comes out with no skirt on, I remove my shirt and pants. We start making out again. She removes her shirt, then bra. This whole time, I've been very chill about everything. I haven't been trying to rush things or get nervous about what will happen next. We make out more. I pull off her panties, then my boxers. We keep making out. She asks if I have a condom. I grab one and put it on.

The make out continues as we walk toward the bed. First, she falls back on the bed. Next, I fall on top of her. We climb, so we are fully on the bed. I am still on top of her. I take my dick and feel for her pussy opening, and I put my dick in her vagina.

I fuck her missionary for a few minutes. Then, she gets up and I start fucking her from behind while she's on all fours. She gets on top of me and rides me cowgirl til she cums. After she cums, she whispers that she wants me to cum.

I start fucking her missionary again and pull her hair at the roots and making out with her hard. I kiss the sides of her neck. Finally, I cum too.

In the morning, she gets on me and rides me cowgirl. She presses her pelvic bone into mine while grinding her pelvis in circles. It hurts like hell, but she is moaning and going nuts over doing this grinding, so I shut up and close my eyes and imagine I'm anywhere else to not think about the pain lol. She cums; I don't.

We go in the shower. She washes herself then me. Max and I meet in the main room. We both whisper in excitement about how the night went down. Max says the girls may want to stay a few more days. I figure, it will be fun to practice fucking more.

The girls come out of the rooms, fully dressed. They say they need to get ready for the wedding that is happening in a few hours. Max and I drive the two girls home, and we talk about meeting up after the wedding.

LISA

I see Lisa in front of the club in a green sequin dress; she is walking while looking at her phone. I open her by complimenting her dress. I transition and ask where she is from. She responds where she is from. I say, "That's great!" and high five her. She interlocks her fingers with my hand on the high five. That's a good start for me. Great sign so early in set. I ask how her trip is going.

She says it is okay, but she is annoyed because she just wants to have fun but is having trouble finding her friends. I say, I'm looking for my friends too, and I'm also trying to have fun. She smiles. We talk about what we've done in Vegas so far and then I kiss her. She kisses back. I'm off to a good start…

I ask what she is doing on her phone. She says her friends keep trying to call her, so she is looking for them. I decide to help her try to find her friends (That was dumb, now that I'm thinking about it. I should have talked about other shit and had her forget about her friends). She keeps complaining about her feet and how sore they are. (I should have taken that as the opportunity to take her to her hotel, rather than find the friends, which could have potentially

9

fucked my set up.)

She gets a call from her friend. The rest of the group is only about 100 feet away at another bar. Lisa and I walk over and meet the friends at Sea Horse Bar in Caesar's. They are chill. Turns out everyone in the group aside from one other girl had met Lisa earlier that day. That is good news for me. I meet Lisa's friend from back home and talk to her for a few moments and briefly meet everyone else.

The group wants to go to Hustler Club, I pitch Rhino because I think the group will appreciate me bringing value to them. I'm sitting with my target, trying to figure out how to get out of going to Rhino with her because the interaction will go too long and she'll probably get tired or lose interest in hooking up if we go to the Rhino. Also, Rhino does not bring me closer to my sex location.

The whole group gets up to go to the front of the hotel and get a limo to Rhino. Lisa is having trouble with her heels and complains. I say we should have her change her heels at her hotel before going to Rhino. She says she can't leave her friends.

I pull her aside at the front of Caesar's and say, "I completely understand you want to be with the group, but your feet are killing you. The limo is going take 20 minutes to show up here, so you are going to have to stand in the heels or sit on the cold steps out here until then. I drove here, so I can drive you to your hotel right now. You can change your shoes and then we can go to Rhino, so we will get there at the same time as her friends. Does that make sense?"

She says, "Ok, but I have to tell my friends."

I say, "Then Tell them."

Lisa tells the friends she is going with me. The friends seem to notice. Lisa and I go to my car. I take a back road to her hotel that I know of, thinking that the main street might take too long at 2am when everyone is leaving the club.

I get lost...

The whole car ride back, I'm calm, relaxed, and saying little jokes and asking qualification questions and saying that I love having a Vegas adventure. I park in the back parking lot. In the future, I will valet for the sake of speed and comfort for her.

We get to her room. She goes into the bathroom. I get on the bed, and take off my shoes and belt and jacket. We make out and start rubbing up and down our bodies. We make out some more. I start kissing her neck as article after article of clothing comes off of her and I intermittently. I take a condom out of my pocket. I tear it open and put it on. I go back to more making out and guide my cock to the entrance of her vagina. We continue to make out. Then, I go inside her.

The sex is far from amazing. She only wants to fuck in missionary. She's also not doing much back. Eventually I cum. She lies there after and says that she's not going to go to the Rhino after all. She says I am welcome to stay the night. I think about it and say I should probably take off. (It's still relatively early on a Saturday, so I'd like to game more.)

On the way out, she asks how old I am. I say, "23."

She groans, "Seriously?"

I say, "Yeah, why?"

She says, "I'm 26. Can you say a number that's older than me?"

I pause. Then say, "Um... Sure. I'm 28."

She says, "Phew, thank you. Have a good night."

TRISH

I see a 2 set standing near the dance floor downstairs at Pure. I ask them if I can hang out with them a second and talk shit about other girls with them. They laugh.

I say, "Let's play 'Guess who's a hooker?'" Dotty smiles.

I make friends with Dotty, Trish's friend quickly. Trish is quick to respond to me and is playful back. I have been practicing breaking rapport lots today, so my game is not unstoppable but close when it comes to shooting the shit.

I find out the logistics: The girls are in Vegas for a few days and staying at MGM. They do not have plans later that night or the next day. Everything seems good, I just do not know what to do with the friend...

We hang out for a while. Dotty goes to the bathroom, and Trish and I have isolation. I try to kiss her on the forehead at one point, but Trish pulls away. I figure I am getting too aggressive with my kino, so I will pull it back to less intense stuff. Trish touches me back a few times, so I know she likes me some; I must have been moving too fast.

Dotty asks me where to go the next night. I say Surrender and then have Trish give me her phone number, so we can hang out at Surrender. (I really want the number as a compliance/investment sort of deal because I plan to sleep with Trish that night.) I mention Chateau to them and that I am going there after Pure and invite them to come. They are initially hesitant to come with me, saying I am a stranger. I shrug it off. Then they are cool with coming.

On the way out, there is a drunk guy that Trish goes over to hug Goodbye. He starts following us with his friend. Trish is talking with the drunk on the walk to the parking garage where my car is parked. I stay non-reactive and am more fun and playful than the guy. I think getting confrontational with the guy might blow me out of set, so I keep walking toward the car with Dotty right beside me and Trish talking to the other guy behind me. The guy looks scruffy and is wearing terrible clothes. I figure, he does not have a chance.

I let the guy follow us all the way to the elevators. He even takes the elevator up to the level the car is parked on. I tell him as we are leaving the elevator that he can meet us at Chateau but I will not drive him.

The girls ask why.

I say, "I do not know him."

The girls say, "You've only known us 20 minutes though" (really it'd been at least 45, but I know that detail is not going to change anything).

I say, "Yes that's true. If you wanna stay with him, you are welcome to, but I am going to Chateau. And he cannot come in my car."

I walk to the car, (all of this is stated as fact, not reaction). Dotty follows me, then Trish spends a few minutes with the guy (probably exchanging numbers) and comes in the car with me.

I think about coming up with a reason to bring the girls

back to the place instead of going to Chateau now that we are in the car, but I am nervous and it does not feel like the girls will be on board after I made them ditch this guy. It is early in the interaction, and I do not want to screw things up; plus, this friend is still here...

So, we go to Chateau. I drive and go to Valet because the walk from the parking garage is too long for a girl in heels to do without being furious by the end. I am hoping one of the hosts I know will be working tonight, so I can look good by having the hosts help me get in.

One of the hosts is there, and he is amazing. The second he sees me with two chicks, he put on a huge smile, comes over toward me, high fives me and acts like I'm his best friend from years and years ago. I am excited with his reaction. He writes me a pass to get everyone in free. As we are walking up the steps inside, Dotty says, "Ok. That was really smooth." (First time I've been called "smooth" in my life. I'll take that as a compliment.)

At Chateau, I take the girls to the balcony because the roof deck is closed. They think the club is very pretty. Dotty buys us all a drink. She takes off to go to the bathroom. I sit with Trish. Trish and I talk about emotionally charged things, like the feeling you get from riding a wave when surfing. I hold eye contact with her for a while and looked at her lips then lean forward. She leans in too. We kiss.

With the kiss taken care of, I know that I am good as long as the pull is smooth. Really the rest of the night is concerned with me making sure the Dotty likes me, which is not too hard. I still am trying to figure out what is going to happen with Dotty in this set. I want to find a wing at Chateau to help me out. I am talking to Trish about the MGM to figure out logistics of whether to go there or to my place. She says, Dotty had a no boys allowed in the room policy…. That settles that question.

I start talking about us all grabbing drinks at my house. I do not DHV the house by saying it is a mansion with 11 bedrooms and a hot tub because I do not want to sound like I am bragging. Trish is fine with the idea of going to my place.

I have 2 options: 1) make Dotty happy with me being alone with Trish or 2) have Dotty come back to the place with me. I let the two girls talk a moment to figure things out.

Once, there is another dude talking to Dotty. I am excited for a moment thinking I have a wing that will help with the set by gaming Dotty. I introduce myself and asked if he is cool bringing the girls to my place. He agrees. I tell him to go for Dotty. He is too drunk and too aggressive with Dotty. He keeps trying to make out with her. His chances of getting with Dotty are done. Dotty eventually agrees to let Trish leave with me, so it all works out.

Trish and I leave the club with Dotty. Dotty hugs Trish Goodbye. The ride back, I am playing music, and Trish is talking. It was a short ride home.

Trish is impressed by the place, and asked if I'd ever read _The Game_.

I ask, "Yeah, a long time ago. Why?"

She says the house reminds her of it.

I laugh inside and say, "That it is a funny observation, and I can see why you would say that."

We go to the bar. I pour a drink, and we cheers to Las Vegas and Neil Strauss (her touch). She also jokes about back-handed compliments. She says they do not work. I am amused because I am thinking of the different ways I broke rapport on her throughout the set.

She asks about me. There is some comfort building where I tell her about my passions. I tell her about stand up comedy and what it means to me... Then, I bring her into my room to show her a stand up comedy video of mine.

Shortly after that, we have sex.

Now, she is laying next to me... I guess, I'll have sex with her again in the morning!

MADISON

Max opens a tall cute girl named Alyssa in front of Marquee. We're in front of the club and the is slowing down for the night. I talked to Alyssa a sec when Max introduces me. Then, I see a cute girl next to her Madison. I open Madison by saying, "What do you think of my hair? I just had sex, and I want to make sure other girls will not notice."

She does not respond. I figure I'll probably always get that reaction when I ask that type of question but shrug off her disinterest.

Next, I say, "It looks like you're waiting for someone, but you look kind of spacey."

Again, not much of a reaction, but I continue. I ask who she is with. She says she is with Alyssa, another guy who seems weird to me, and two people she is in a fight with who are still inside Marquee.

Madison tells me she is from Wisconsin.

I tease by saying, "Oh wow… Wisconsin. I'm sorry to hear that."

I ask some qualifier. She says she lives in LA now, but her office moved to SF.

I look her up and down and say she has too much color on to be from LA to break rapport again. Then, I ask what she'll do in SF. She answers.

I give her a fist bump that I call the SF Earthquake Shake. It starts as a first bump but when our knuckles touch, we both shake our hands shake really quick then have them drop, like a building fell in an earthquake. Madison says that was dumb. I ask how long she's in town, ignoring her previous comment. She says she is in Vegas til the next night. She is going back to Wisconsin for Thanksgiving. I guess that she is the middle child. She says I'm right (generally, I'm correct 75% of the time with these reads: oldest, youngest, or middle and what type of siblings they have).

I ask if she's close to her family. She says yeah.

I ask for her number because we have to hang out when she's in Las Vegas (Now, I know that I don't have a solid reason to grab the number, but I am working on this still) She hands me her phone. I put in my info and have her text me her name (Madison), so she is texting me first. She goes to the bathroom.

While she is gone, there is a drunk guy running back and forth at the entrance to Marquee throwing dollar bills into the air singing "We're off to see the Wizard." While other people are confused with what the hell is going on, me and the janitor are picking up the money. I grab $14.

When Madison comes out from the bathroom, I fan the money out and tell her what happened and say we have to do shots to celebrate (except I sing it as "Shots, shots, shots, shots…." like the LMFAO song).

Madison and I go to chandelier bar which is close but downstairs, so it's out of eye sight of the rest of the group. We order a drink then sit. I ask more qualifiers about how she got her job, then I hit on her family again and ask who she is closer to, her mother or father. She invests a little about being closer to her father. She tells me about her relationship with her mom.

A few times when she gives less investment, I break rapport. I think am verbally rewarding her investment very well. I say "Very cool" quite a few times. My kino is awkward. I actually see her respond negatively when I touch her by being slightly jumpy.

So far, I have told her almost nothing about me, except that I am on mini-retirement as a description to my current occupation. She doesn't seem concerned.

She rolls her eyes every now and again when I reward her, but I figure I'll just ignore that and continue rewarding as I have been. Mike comes into the set. He is talking about going to the Rhino. It is about time I bounce her outside of this hotel, so I say to her, "Let's go to Rhino."

She is sitting, so I go over to Mike to see what I am supposed to do to get her to go. He tells me to lead, so I grab Madison's arm and gently pull her from her sitting position in Chandelier bar to move toward the car. Madison, Alyssa, and the weird dude Madison's chauffeuring around come with us. They get in the car (I parked right by the elevator. That made buying temp remain high).

We get to Rhino, Madison goes to the bathroom. Everyone sits. When Madison gets back, I realize I need to isolate her again from her friends. I tell her we're going to the other bar away from where everyone else is to see my friend who's working. Again, I do what I did at Chandelier Bar and grab her by the wrist and lead her. We switch to arm-in-arm going to the bar. I have already tried to kiss Madison in Cosmo, and she pulled away. When she pulled away, she said that she was not going to kiss me since I had already had sex that night.

I decide I will continue with the interaction before I try to kiss her again (and I note not to bring up sex with other women in set again). We go to the other bar. We both order a drink. She points out that I'm not paying for her drink. I ignore it (in my head, I start realizing that i can use the bar at our place as an excuse to pay her back with shots at our place).

The bartender and I are getting along and shooting the shit. I figure, this makes me look good since I said I had a friend at the bar. It also shows that I am a social person.

Madison starts telling me about her brother dying. I know this is the point toward deeper investment. I tell her how impressive it is to hear about this story and ask what it is like to no longer have her brother. She tells me about how her family notices his absence around the holidays most. She lists the holidays that they miss him at. It's deep. I kiss her on the forehead. Had she not pulled back earlier, I would have kissed her on the lips.

Max comes up and ask if we want to go to the house. I say, "That's cool. I owe Madison 'Shots, shots, shots, shots…'"

She's cool with going too. We leave the Rhino. I link arm-in-arm with her again. This time, she squeezes tightly on my arm. I know the investment I just got was deep. I yell to Max when we get to the parking lot to have the weird dude, Alyssa, and Max go in his car.

That leave me alone with Madison in my car. I open the door for her when we get to my car. She says, "Thank you."

I nod then close her door. I walk around and get in on the driver side. Once we're in the car, I know I need to kiss her before we go to the house. I lean to kiss her across the center console. She kisses back. Immediately after, she says she will not sleep with me because I've already slept with a girl tonight. I ignore this.

We get to the house. I don't give a tour. I walk over to the bar and pour us a drink. We play the arcade video game we have in the other room. She likes that.

Earlier in the night, I mentioned I will be a famous comic someday, and she gave me shit about it, saying I wasn't funny. I said would have to show her my stand up video later to seed a justification to bring her into my room later in the night.

So, after the video game, I say, "Hey! I still need to show you that stand up comedy video! I seriously am funny."

She comes with me into my room to see the video. Madison tells me her friend is leaving for the airport in a 30 minutes, and she will have to go soon to say "Goodbye."

I say, "That's fine. You guys will see each other shortly."

I don't try to solve the problem. I just acknowledge it and move on. Inside the room, we make out heavy while we are sitting on the bed with my laptop also sitting on the bed. After a few minutes of making out, I rub her pussy. I know, I do not have a lot of time to escalate, so I'm escalating at the best pace I can without triggering LMR.

A few more minutes later, I'm fingering her. I'm circling my middle finger inside her. She grabs for my dick, which is not hard yet. I tell her to help me get hard. She starts straddling me (she's wearing a skirt, so I don't even have to take any clothes off). And grinding on me. From where I'm lying, I look up to see her wet pussy lips peaking from the side of her thong. That gets me rock hard. As I feel her wet lips and the small amount of material from her thong rub up and down my dick, I know I need to put a condom on now or I'm going to be too horny in a second to think, and

I'll be tempted to put it in raw.

I pull a condom from my pants and put it on. She grabs my dick, rises several inches, so her pussy is on the tip of my dick then slowly slides down, sitting on my dick with me now inside her. Feels amazing.

She's riding me. It's not more than a few minutes, and she cums. Her pussy get tight on my dick and that makes me cum.

We sit for a second both reeling in how quickly everything escalated. The noise of other people outside brings us back to the moment. We realize she has to say "Goodbye" to her friend and the weird dude is in the living room with Alyssa and Max. Madison and I quickly make ourselves more presentable then leave the room. I drive everyone home.

Later that day, Madison texts about meeting up after the holiday.

SHA

I am not in an amazing mood, and I head to the bathroom on the second floor of Cosmo across from Marquee hoping that splashing some water on my face will knock me out of my funk and get my head in a better place. I never make it to the bathroom. 20 feet before the bathroom, I see Sha is sitting on the floor leaning against the wall.

I make an observation, "Wow! Someone is having fun in Vegas!" as a joke because she is clearly not having fun and put out my hand to high five her.

She tells me to sit next to her. (It's after 3 am by the way) Right then, I know that we are going to have sex, as long as I play my cards right. Good mood or bad mood, Sha's interest perks me up.

I find out more about her situation. She says she is waiting for friends who are in the bathroom. She is staying at Planet Hollywood, and leaving in a day or two. Her friends are staying in the room with her. I figure, her place is not ideal. She also says she has a rule with her friends not to leave the Cosmo. I am not sure what that means, but I figure that my place may not work. I quickly run through other solutions and think that my car could be an option.

Security says we can't sit in the hallway, so we go to the bench by Chandelier Bar. Her friends come out. I introduce myself. After talking to the friends for about 1 minute, they tell us to have fun and disappear.

Sha says she wants to get a drink at Chandelier bar. That's fine by me. We go there, and my focus for the conversation is comfort. We talk about jobs and life.

After about 30 minutes, her friends come by again, and the guy tells Sha to "fuck me good and represent SD well."

He tells me to get Sha drunk. They walk off. I smile and say nothing throughout all of this. There is nothing to argue with and anything I say will make it worse, so I just shut up.

My car is parked below Vesper bar. Sha wants another drink, so I figure we may as well go in the direction that leads to my car. Sha and I bounce to Vesper bar. I ask if she's ready to go. She says 1 more drink. I pay for the beers; she paid for the round at Chandelier Bar. I start asking sexual qualifiers.

I ask, where is the craziest place she had sex, where is the craziest place she had sex in Vegas.

Then, I ask, "Are you adventurous?"

She says, "Yes."

I say, "Let's go on an adventure."

I grab her by the wrist and lead her to the elevator. Once we get to the car, I open the door to the back seat, and put down the seats, so there is more room to have sex. The car sex is not ideal comfort-wise and some people are walking by, but it's fun!

AURORA

I go up to Aurora at the bar. She's a skinny pale girl in a black dress and say, "You're really skinny. Do you have a high metabolism or do you throw up a lot?"

She laughs and says, "High Metabolism."

I high five her and ask where she's from.

She says, "Poland."

I try to be funny and say, "I love Polish sausages."

I ask where she is staying. She says, "A hotel."

I break rapport because she does not qualify with the name of the hotel.

I ask who she is in the club with.

She is there by herself.

I ask when she's leaving Vegas.

She is leaving the next day at 5pm.

I am having a lot of trouble hearing her with both the noise, her soft voice, and her Polish accent. I tell her a few times to speak English to be funny, but she does not think I am funny.

I ask another qualifier, and I can't hear her answer. I can see she is beginning to get frustrated when I can't understand her, so I realize that I need to fix this language barrier.

I take out my phone and start communicating with her through my Notepad. First, I have her type her name, so I know who the hell she is.

I type "Do you want to dance?" because I want to kiss and sexually escalate, and I am having trouble escalating the conversation.

She types, "Yes, after another drink."

I don't exactly understand whether she is blowing me off or telling me that she needs another drink in order to go out and dance. As I'm in doubt, I side with the latter determination since the former throws me out of set.

Her body language throughout the first ten minutes is very difficult to understand. She is constantly turning back and forth, leaning her stomach against the bar or her back against the bar and is always about a foot away from me, except when she leans in to tell me something. I mirror her body language against the bar because I don't want to convey more interest to her than she is showing to me.

I'm breaking a lot of rapport. I tell her that I feel like if I poked her with my finger, she'd fall over.

I show her pics of my dog and me and my sister with the easter bunny, since I realize that I can't talk effectively to her, and I want to see if those pics will help out at all.

She tells me she had a golden retriever and that she knows about the easter bunny.

She leaves the back bar inside Chateau and walks through the dance floor to the other side where she posts up again. I follow right behind her.

When I get there, I ask her what she does.

I still can't understand her, so I take out my phone. I use the Notepad on it to ask questions and get her responses.

I type to ask her what she's doing in Chateau by herself.

At some point I ask what's something crazy she's done in Vegas. Somehow, I find out that she's had sex with an Aussie at his hotel in Vegas. That tells me she is willing to be pulled to my sex location.

I decide to bite the bullet and go sexual. I ask how old she was when she first kissed a guy. She says 14. I ask how old she was when she first had sex. She will not answer.

I type in the Notepad, over or under 15. She signals higher. I guess 17. She says lower. I say 16.

I type in Notepad, "What is the craziest place you have had sex."

She types, "Trampoline."

I type, "Where would you like to have sex?"

She types, "A cozy bed."

I type, "Is your bed cozy?"

She types, "Not really."

I type, "Haha, Mine is ;p"

She types, "Later."

At this point, part of me is convinced we're going to fuck, and I just need to wait. The other part of me doesn't know what is happening.

I type, "Do you want to dance in a bit."

She say, "I need another drink. Do what I want and find me in a while."

I do not know what this really means. I stick around. I type "Do you drink a lot?"

She says, "Sometimes."

I begin to type a response, but she will never read it. She takes off and is headed in the direction of the bar I met her at. I follow her. On the way, I bump into Max. I tell him I don't know what is going on. He tells me Aurora is showing bad body language.

I say, "Yeah, but she's investing. I'm confused."

He says, "Let's go do other sets."

I'm content to leave.

Thirty minutes later, I've gamed a few other sets in the club. The club is quickly slowing down. Out of nowhere, Aurora runs up to me and says, "Save me!"

I look around to make sure I'm not crazy. Yep. She's talking to me. I say, "Ok. I'm leaving. Do you want to come?"

She nods, "Yes."

I have not kissed her yet, so I say, "I'm going back to my place in my car. Is that fine with you?" She agrees again.

I shrug and think, Works for me…

The way home, I am trying to make small talk with her. I talk about Vegas and the things to do in Vegas, and I ask about her home. Finally, she says, "Stop! Will you please stop talking? We are just going to have sex! Ok."

Her forwardness takes me off guard, but apparently she's on board with the sex, so… I turn on the music, and there's no talking the rest of the way. When we get to the place, I have her take off her shoes by the door and we walk into my room.

There are bunk beds in the room. She does not seem to care. Standing there inside the room, I try to kiss her. She turns her head. She whispers, "No kissing."

She unbuttons my pants and undoes my belt. She pulls my pants to my knees and drops down to her knees all in one motion… She's good…

I sigh as her lips go around my cock. She is sucking up and down on my dick for a few minutes. I'm turned on as shit. A girl who just does the thing! This is great!

I take my hands and pull her upwards by her elbows then walk her several feet over to the bed. She lies down. I take out a condom and put it on. I don't even take off her clothes at first. She's wearing a dress. I start massaging her pussy underneath her dress. She's wet. I spit on my hand for some extra lube. I put the spit between her pussy lips as I move my middle finger and ring finger up and down her pussy.

A few minutes later, I finger her. She is unimaginably wet inside. I'm so turned on. She tells me to put my dick inside her. I'm not going to disagree with that. I take out a condom and put it on.

I enter her. She feels amazing. I begin thrusting. Slowly then quicker. She wants to be on top. We switch positions while I stay inside her. Now, she is on top, working me amazingly. A few minutes later, it's back to me on top. She's moaning and thrusting and shaking. The bed is creaking. I cum. She feels me cumming and that sets her off. After I cum, I just stay inside her a few minutes. Then, I go and wash off.

While we're lying next to each other after sex, I ask why she told me to save her. She told me there was another guy who wouldn't leave her alone that she didn't want to be around. I asked if she was actually planning to leave with me when she said she would earlier. She nodded yes. We had sex again after that.

I dropped her off at her hotel the next morning.

ANGEL

I am sitting on the table at Cathouse talking to a girl when Max comes over with two girls, one on each side and says, "Chris, meet my new friends."

I turn from the girl I'm talking to and introduce myself to the 2 girls. At first, I assume his target is Angel because she is hotter than her friend Libby in my opinion. I find out where they are from.

Quickly, it becomes apparent that I am supposed to be talking to Angel. Max is already making out with Libby and sits down next to her. I've talked to Angel for all of 1 or 2 minutes when she gets up to go to the bathroom.

I go to the bathroom too, seeing as I don't want to sit there while Max and Libby are making out. When Angel comes back, I ask some logistical questions about where they were that night. She says they were in LAX, and she hates LAX.

I note to myself not to say that I work for LAX. We end up talking about what drives us and what we want to do with our lives. Angel tells me about how she is into music and DJing but has a corporate marketing job, and at the end of the day she doesn't know what she wants to do. She asks me why I live in Vegas now. I want to build comfort by showing vulnerability, so I show her a picture of me as an eight grader where I look fat and dorky and I say that I always used to do well in school, that I was a big nerd, and that I never had the fun I wanted to growing up. I say that I went to a good college and thought that after I got a good job, everything would improve, but at the end of the day, I had the education and the job and still wasn't happy, so I left my job and moved to Vegas with friends, and now I promote clubs.

I say, in 5-10 years I will be a nationally known comedian touring the country, and this Vegas experience is the next rung on the ladder to get there. It is a means to an end. (Later, Angel tells me that she liked when I said that I wanted to be a comedian because it is interesting and something unique that is more than just a story about being a nerd. She also liked that I said promoting was a means to an end because it inferred I didn't want to be a promoter when I was 35 years old.)

About 20 minutes after meeting these girls, Max announces we're taking off. I haven't kissed Angel yet, but I know the pull is on. Max is running this set, so I don't have to kiss Angel yet since Max already has been kissing Libby. Max has been kissing Libby too much in my opinion, and my texts telling him to calm down are not changing anything.

We took a car to the club, but Max is walking toward the taxi line. I figure, he either spoke to Libby and realized she does not want to go in our car or he's taking the taxi as insurance to prevent any last minute resistance toward the pull. I shut up and let Max take the lead.

We all squeeze into the back of the taxi, so there is 4

across. Sure, there is room in the driver seat, but I know that will create a psychological barrier between Anel and I, which will hurt rapport; if we sit next to each other (even if it's cramped), it will help rapport.

The whole ride back, Max and Libby are heavily making out. I'm talking to Angel about the trip and a bunch of random light stuff to take the focus off Max and LIbby. She is responding. Not much but some.

I'm nervous the heavy make out will blow things for Max, but no way to stop the make out since he is not checking the texts I'm sending him and telling him to calm down in front of the girls is a sure way to ruin the set. Talking in front of them about the set will look too calculating and freak them out.

We get to the place. The gate is not opening. We ring the buzzer, but no one responds. There's a brief moment of panic between Max and I as we look at each other as to what to do next…

The taxi driver starts to talk. I know, he's going to suggest we go somewhere else… Not good for the set. We're at the entrance to the sex location. No going back in set now.

I say, "Thanks. We're good."

I take out cash to pay the guy. I don't even know how much the cab is, but I give at least $10 more than the ride. I say, "Here. Keep the change. Have a good night."

We're all out of the cab, looking at the gate. Max messaged everyone we live with to open the gate. No response. I say, "Looks like we have to climb!"

We walk to the fence and climb over. It's not too high. Libby doesn't care at all. Angel is not thrilled but is going along with it.

Angel says, "Do you guys even live here?"

"Shh," I say. "You'll wake the neighbors."

Not exactly the most reaffirming thing that I could say, but if the neighbors wake up with us climbing over the fence and call the cops, well… that's a state break I don't need to deal with… Plus, the neighbors already hate us for the loud parties and hearing girls moaning in the hot tub in the back yard at 4am.

We hop the fence. It's not as bad as I thought it would be and walk to the place. The girls are impressed with the size.

Once we're inside, Max makes a beeline for his room with Libby. "Well done," I think to myself.

Now, it's me and Angel in the main room. I haven't kissed her yet. Strike that. I haven't even gotten mediocre investment yet. She did not say much at the club. And now, she is closed off with her body language and her short answers to my qualifiers. I am annoyed that I cannot get through her exterior. If this were my set, I would start peppering her with breaks in rapport to see if that would incite her to want to qualify more. But this isn't my set. Max is in the other room, and he's close to getting his dick wet, so I cannot risk saying something that could potentially sever the set with Angel and make her mad enough to grab Libby and want to leave. I would be the worst wing ever.

So, it's time to play "Nice Guy Game." Until I get the "all clear" from Max that he's gotten it in and I can risk severing with Angel, I am going to make sure she is comfortable and not stir any waves that would make her want to leave (which would likely mean her taking Libby too).

I sit on the sofa across from Angel since and mirror her behavior. She is on her phone, so I get on mine. As I am pretending to be on my phone doing anything, I continue to ask low investment qualifiers. I focus on the current trip and plans for the remainder of the weekend. Angel responds. Not much but she is giving me something at least.

Then, Angel asks if I have any food. I do not, but I figure there has to be something to eat in the fridge. I check the fridge and freezer. There are corn dog bites in the freezer. They aren't mine, but we have a rule in the house: If it's for game, nothing is off limits… just replace it after.

I ask if corn dog bites are fine for her. She says, "Yes."

I microwave the food, put them on a plate, and get her mustard and ketchup. I'm not particularly hungry (especially for corn dog bites), but eating with her will build rapport and show that I didn't cook the corn dog bites solely for her. I eat a few too. We talk a little more as we are eating. There's always the general talk about how we all know each other. The general answer (unless Max and I have a random backstory worked out for a set) is that we met through mutual friends and are just a bunch of cool dudes living together. We finish eating. I pick up the plate and bring it to the sink and place it in the sink. I'll wash it later. Just putting it in the sink builds some attraction points because it shows I take pride in the place I live by keeping it clean.

Then Angel says, "Not to sound like a slut, but where's your room?"

That took me off guard. Things are going better than I realized. Obviously, I'm not going to complain, so I say, "Follow me."

We walk the 20 feet to get to my room. I close the door. We start making out. That turns to undressing. I figure I can take time a little building up to sex: since she basically just agreed to sex when she asked where my room is, undressing her and having foreplay will be fine too…

The making out continues as we remove each article of clothing til we are both naked. I love her body. Nice sized tits. Black hair with blue streaks. A tattoo on side of her rib cage. Sexy.

I caress in between her legs with my right hand. She is jerking me off. I don't think I could be more hard with 10 Viagra pills in me. I'm amazed at how smooth she is down below. It's nice…

I can feel her hard clit. She's not wet all on the outside of her pussy. I stick my finger between her pussy lips. Super slick and slimy! All right! Enough foreplay! Time to fuck!

We are both on the bed at this point. She was straddling me during part of the foreplay, but now it's time to fuck. I turn to reach from a condom from my pants pocket that is on the floor by the bed. I push her off of me and grab her by her hips and guide her, so she is lying in the middle of the bed with her head on my pillow in the missionary position, feet on the bed and knees bent, pointing into the air. Her legs are spread wide. I put a condom on my dick and hold it at the entrance to her vagina a moment. I take the head and guide it up and down from the top to the bottom of her pussy. She is so wet. What a turn on.

Then, I stick it in.

Sex is a lot of fun with Angel. Best position with her is when her ass is in my groin and we are lying in a sort of spooning position. It's great access to her pussy, takes a lot of the cardio work away and feels amazing. (Plus, I like her ass)

She cums quick then is super sensitive, so I stay inside her hard and hold steady. Feels amazing. We start talking

(New for me to talk with my dick still inside a girl, but the type of new activity I can get used to). We are talking about when Angel started liking me. She admits she hated me most of the time.

"Don't get me wrong," Angel say. "I'm a closed off bitch to most people I meet. It's easier that way. Plus, it's fun to fuck with people and see how they respond."

I say, "So why didn't you like me?"

Angel says, "Well, at first I thought you were a prick because you ditched that chick you were talking to when you met us, like she was no one. Then, you say you work for club, and I think 'Great. Another one of these guys.' Also, you said some pretty dick-ish things right when I met you. To be honest, the only reason I let you fuck me is because you made the corn dogs. I figured if you were willing to make some person you didn't know corn dogs even when it was clear you weren't going to get any, you probably weren't a complete asshole."

All good feedback for me. Anyhow, Angel is in Vegas a few times a year, so it will be cool to hopefully see her again.

PAULA

I'm in Surrender nightclub. It's Industry Night. Yeah, I'm still tired (I was up til like 10am to close the flight attendant then slept about an hour before I had to start work), but hell I'm on it! Let's do it again tonight!

First walk through of the club, I'm not fully warmed up, but there's still plenty of time. I am headed toward the back bar to meet up with a few wings when I see a cute slender blonde walking in the direction opposite from me. There's no direction to her walk, so I know she's lost. To top it off, she has an empty champagne glass in her hand. There's a chance she's a girl that was at one of these tables; it's more likely though that a promoter hooked her up with the free champagne for getting in under his name on the guestlist. Good news is, the free drinks cut off 20 minutes ago, so offering to grab a drink with her (if that's the route I choose to take) will hit better than if I offered to grab a drink when she could get them for free from the bar.

Asking if she needs help will be an easy observational open that provides value. Odds of her responding positively and receptively are like 99%. I open by pressing the fingers of my left hand against her upper arm. I say, "Hey you look lost. Do you need help finding something?"

She turns to me, and it looks like I knocked her out of her searching state. She refocuses her attention on me and says that she is lost.

I ask, "What she's looking for?"

Paula says, "Either the exit or another drink."

She continues walking in the direction she was headed before I opened her. Well, no sense in me going to meet my wings when there's a set right here… I pivot, so I'm faced in the same direction as her and take a few quick strides to get in front of her. Even though she is continuing her pace with or without me, I am leading once I get in front and she is chasing me (even if unintentionally at first).

I say, "Cool. Follow me."

We're leaving the outside portion of the club and heading toward the exit. I figure, I'll settle both of her interests at once: I'll get her outside the club and grab a drink with her. Leaving the club means less distractions (and less interruptions from the people she came with). Grabbing a drink will give me time to elicit investment and build attraction.

As we're walking through the club, I focus on logistics. First, I ask who she is there with. I want to know if there is going to be any resistance that I haven't anticipated to leaving the club because she doesn't want to ditch her friends. She tells me that she is with a group of people but doesn't know or care where they are. Interesting answer. That means one of two things to me: Option 1) She got in a fight with her friends and I have a brief window to capitalize on her not being thrilled with them before the reconciliation process or Option 2) they are coworkers or some other form of acquaintance where she really does not care about them. I'll ask a follow up to the group dynamics based on her other answers.

I ask where she is staying. She says the Westin. Interesting answer. That's where the stewardess from earlier today was staying…

I ask how long she is in town. She says 24 hours. Interesting answer. That's how long the stewardess from earlier today was staying…

I ask what she does for work. She says she works for British Airways.

I start laughing to myself and try to not let my amusement shine through. Can you say, Deja Vu?!

I already know all of her logistics! I learned from the British Airways chick last night! Every British Airways employee gets their own room at the Westin. She will not be leaving until late the next day. This is too funny!

We are at the exit to Surrender. There's always that weird sobering up feeling that hits when leaving the club. The brightness, the quiet, the lack of chaos. It's easy to let that kill the set right there. And it's easy to do, seeing as she and I have only been in set a few minutes. Before there's any time to assess everything, I lead us toward Eastside Bar, the closest bar near the club that usually has available seating. There's nothing special about it. It's not a bar I would have more than one drink at. It's definitely not the type of bar to gain more than mid-level investment, but it's close and I do not plan to stay in the casino awhile. I just want to be here long enough to build enough rapport that she is comfortable bouncing to a bar outside of the hotel with me.

I tell her, "Let's grab a drink."

I'm already walking in the direction of Eastside Bar. I am about half a stride in front of her. She agrees. I reward her by saying it's great she is independent and willing to take on Vegas.

Even though I know from yesterday that the British Airways personnel have their own hotel room, I confirm with Paula that she is not sharing her room with anyone (can't be too careful) by saying, "It's actually really cool that British Airways hooks you up when you come to Vegas. They still give you your own room, right?"

She nods.

I say, "Yeah. That's cool because then you don't have to deal with an annoying roommate who snores or something." I say this second part to ground why I asked if she was in the room by herself, so that it does not sound like I'm some uncover agent trying to case a joint.

When we get to Eastside Bar. There are only 2 seats together that are available and next to each other. Problem is, the chairs are not the same height… That height differential is going to screw up the whole set. No being suave with kino or the kiss if I need to bend down or stand up to kiss her, not to mention all of the incidental touching while she is investing that will go out the window. It's a risk, but I think I can bounce her from the hotel to the back bar at Peppermill right now. She has already invested easily and come with me outside the club hardly knowing me. If I pitch Peppermill to her in a way that does not put a lot of pressure on it, she will probably come. Also, Peppermill will give me more isolation, I can go deeper into investment, and it's on the way to the house if I determine my place is a better sex location that the Westin.

I ask, "Hey, have you ever been to the Peppermill?"

Odds are close to zero she has gone. Of course, she says, No. I say, "Ok. 24 hours in Vegas? You have to check it out before you go. It's literally right next door and has the true Vegas feel. Want to check it out instead of this crowded bar?"

She agrees to go.

We already walked past one of the parking garage entrances to the parking garage (the one right by Surrender's exit). Even though that is the most direct route to the car, I have us walk a slightly longer way to get to my car, so we do not go backwards in set. If she feels like we are retracing steps, she may question whether I know where I'm going, which could hurt the rapport I've built so far and make her less likely to get in the car with me. I also haven't mentioned I drove yet, so I need to nail potential objections before they come up. I say, "You already drank tonight?"

Paula says, "A little."

I say, "I'm jealous. I haven't drank yet. I'm excited for the Peppermill, so I get to FINALLY drink."

I hope saying that will eliminate the objection that she cannot get in the car with me because she is afraid I am drunk. On the walk toward the car, the conversation is light and playful. We are talking mostly of travel and places we want t go. I pretend to be jealous about all the places she gets to go. The conversation is lively even as we are walking through the parking lot. That's a good sign.

We get to the car. I open the door for her, there is no resistance in getting into my car. I get in and keep the conversation going as I'm backing out and heading to the Peppermill. I cannot remember what I said on the ride over. That part of my verbal game basically goes on autopilot. My standard play in the car is to repeat what she says back to me with more enthusiasm then to reword the sentence in a way that has a misinterpretation in it that I can then break rapport on.

We get to the Peppermill, and I lead her to the fire pit. The fire pit is sexy, secluded and forces close contact. Now that we are both sitting in front of the fire pit, I know I need to qualify Paula. I ask a whole ton of questions including: What is it like traveling all the time? Does she ever feel alone? Does she feel like she's found herself because of being alone? How many brothers and sisters does she have? Does she like dogs? What was she like in high school? How many relationships has she been in? Who ended her relationships?

I don't know how much of this investment is necessary for a one night stand that seems fairly in the bag, but I'm going to be safe and go deep rather than sorry and try to close without playing the full game.

The cocktail waitress comes over. I see a brief look of surprise from her when she sees me with a different chick than last night, but she is getting used to seeing me with different girls by this point. We both order a drink. I pay since I am the one who suggested grabbing drinks, and Paula already invested into the interaction by bouncing with me to Peppermill.

I realize a few times that I'm showing too much interest in my body language. I reorient my body to face more away from her, so it looks like she was more attracted to me than I am to her. When I pull her in for a hug, Paula's whole body falls into me, which is an indicator she is comfortable with me. The feedback from the kino is different than the investment her body is giving me; her legs are turned away from me, so I am unsure how well I am really doing in the set.

The next time she qualifies midlevel, I kiss her on the forehead. She allows me. That is a good sign, but still... this body language!! So confusing. I offer her a high five for a reward, she slaps it with a smirk on her face. It's obvious she's having fun. Good sign. I put out my hand again and pretend to pull it back quickly. She waits with a strategic look on her face and slaps my hand when I let it sit a few seconds too long. Then, I put out both hands. A bigger grin goes across her face as she slaps both. I slap up as she's slapping down. We get into a sort of slap battle where I'm moving my hands up and down and she's hitting them as quickly as she can. It reminds me of the Whack-a-Mole game at the arcade. With all of this BT in the air, I see my window to kiss. There's a split second pause, and I kiss her. She kisses back. It's on!

I have hardly invested so far. It's time to change gears; comfort is a two-way street. Like she is reading my mind, she takes my phone and starts looking through the photos on it. I have already shown her a picture of me as a fat kid, so the photo album on my iPhone is set to the comfort pictures of me: me as a child, me with family, my pets, me working in the woods. Then she opens up my Facebook app. There is a message from a friend thanking me for helping him get into clubs. Everything she sees is either a DHV or a comfort builder. Kinda lucky that she did not see any pictures of me being a manwhore. In the future, I will be more strategic about what a chick will see if she snoops on my phone.

I mention going back to her place, she asks what we will do. I do not have a good response (being direct will put too much pressure on everything, but I did not spend time earlier seeding a reason to go to her place), so I stay quiet for a moment. Then, it hits me! I ask if she has alcohol in her room. I tell her that I would like to have another drink with her, but I do not want to drive right after drinking because it is not be safe, so we can go to her place.

She agrees and says there's a bar downstairs. I will concede to the bar downstairs if I have to, but I will try to come up with a reason to get back to her room once we are there.

We get in the car again, and I head to the Westin. As we're getting there, she talks about how much cooler her car is than mine. I know she is right. The Subaru is definitely not a chick mobile, but I appreciate the easy conversation to be light and playful where I playfully argue with her about why my car is awesome. The debate ends with me opening up the moonroof. She puts her head out the window going down Flamingo with the Strip in view. She is loving it.

We park and I am curious with where we are going to end up; it's either her room or the bar downstairs… I am walking in front as I follow her movement from behind me to make sure I am leading the right way. The elevators are directly in front. The bar is to the left. She is half a step behind me to my right. She has not started to veer left yet. I keep walking to the elevator. She follows.

We get into the elevator. She presses the button to her room. I have not justified a reason to go up to her room. Why say anything when things are already in motion, right?

Paula mentions something about playing a casino game. I tell her the game sounds fun, and we will play in a little bit. We go up to her room. When we're in her room, she starts to clear off her bed. I'm very aware that it's on, and I stand a moment and wait. She turns back toward me. We hold eyes. I move my face in to bridge the foot gap between us. We start making out. 15 seconds into the make out, I am rubbing my hands all over her torso, pressing her toward the bed. She walks back 2 steps until the backs of her legs touch the bed. She fall back and grabs my shirt taking me with her.

She is frantically trying to unbutton my shirt. I continue making out with her while pulling off her sweater. Then, I get on the bed and reposition her by grabbing her upper arms, so she is on top. It's easier to take off her clothes when she is on top. I pull off her shirt and bra. I unbutton my shirt (she is having trouble) while she undoes my belt and jeans.

While I takeoff my pants, she takes off hers. I get back on top. From making out, I work my mouth down to her breasts. I am lightly sucking and gently nibbling her nipples and the areola. Her eyes are closed. There are occasional moans coming from her. She turns her head, so the side of her neck is more exposed. I move up from playing with her nipples to lightly biting and kissing her neck. I note to be gentle: no marks. Marks can lead to buyer's remorse because she has to deal with covering them up and questions she may be embarrassed to answer. Even though I know she will be gone tomorrow and the odds of repeat sex are not in my favor, no sense in leaving her with any regrets of hooking up with me. Does not seem like good karma either.

I change focus. I kiss down her body to her thighs. I am not actually kissing her pussy, but I am getting close. She keeps gripping my back and buttocks firmly. Her fingernails are digging into my back as she scratches up and down me. It hurts, and I wince a little, but I know better than to tell her to stop. That could screw EVERYTHING up.

She is tugging at my boxers, and I help her take them off. She sees how hard I am and starts stroking my dick. It's game time! I go for her panties. She is already on it. She pulls them to her knees, slips one leg out, and kicks the panties across the room with her other leg.

The condom I need to grab is in my pants. I can get off of her and grab it while I'm on top, but that will break state slightly. If I reposition her, so she is on top (a position she was happy to be in a few minutes earlier), I can grab the condom from the pants amidst the movement and not break the sexual state at all. I flip her, so she is back on top of me. We're making out. My dick is erect and the shaft is running up and down her wet slit. All she has to do is move her body an inch forward, and my dick is in paradise. The adrenaline and endorphins and whatever other neurons are getting released during sex are firing at all all time high right now. Paula grabs my dick and lift her leg slightly in the air. She's about to stick it in…

Reluctantly (and I mean VERY reluctantly), I tell her to wait a sec. I grab the condom I took from my pants pocket and put it on. It's a very minor state break but absolutely necessary: I don't care how horny I am, I'm not risking unprotected sex. I put on the condom, and she guides me inside of her. She starts grinding on me. Feels great.

After a few minutes, I flip her and start fucking her missionary, then it's doggy. She wants to get back on top. She stays there about 10 minutes and then slows the grind. I roll her, so I'm back on top, fucking her missionary. She is not nearly as horny as she was a few minutes ago.

She says, "Can you hurry up and cum already?"

I say, "What?"

She says, "I already came. Cum."

I know it's going to be a while before I can cum. The sex

earlier that day promised that. After a few more minutes, she gets off. I shrug and go into the bathroom to throw away the condom and wash my dick. When I come out of the bathroom, she's asleep. I was hoping for a second round. Doesn't look like that's going to happen. No worries. I've still got to finish my field report from the night before. It's only around 1:30am, so I can actually get some sleep before work the next day… I take off.

VANESSA

I am in front of Excalibur promoting for the clubs that night when I see Vanessa walking by. She is walking around, and looking up At the sights. She looks a little lost, and it's not too usual to see a girl alone by herself in the middle of the day. I open her to see what she's up to. Odds of her going to my club are low because she is by herself (As a promoter, single sets of girls are close to useless to talk to because 1) they usually put their guard up assuming you're hitting on them, and 2) girls make decisions of where to go based on the group's consensus, so unless you are talking to the head chick and can convince her to get every other girl in her group on board with your club, it's an uphill battle). All the same, she is a hot girl. There aren't other sets around to promote to. And if she isn't going to the club, maybe I can convert it into something else…

I open Vanessa by pointing out that she looks lost, and I ask where she wants to go. I do not touch her on the open. There is not a lot of congestion on the sidewalk, so touching would be a little awkward. It would be too close too soon; there is a higher chance she would categorize me as a robber than anything else.

She says she is looking for Tropicana.

I point out the hotel. It's just across the street and show how to get there. I figure, "May as well try and pitch my club now."

I take a few quick steps to get in front of Vanessa and walk with her. I start by saying, "While you're on the way, I figure I may as well pitch my clubs and pool parties to you. Want to check them out?"

I make the pitch purposefully not smooth. I find that reluctantly pitching the clubs tends to get a higher response from girls because they don't categorize me as the hype-y promoter that is full of shit. She says, "Sure. Where's there to go?"

I say, "Depends what you like. I'll text you where to go if you want. Honestly, the club I work for sucks tonight, but you get free drinks, and it's right by you. The pool party tomorrow is pretty cool though."

Again, I am more honest with her about where to go because I figure it's her first day here (she didn't know where her hotel was and she was more receptive to me than a girl who has been in Vegas more than a day who starts ignoring every promoter she sees). If I lead her wrong the first day, she will not listen to anything else I say about clubs (so I lose money), and she will not trust me to meet up with her the next few days if my club sucks when I said the club would be good.

Vanessa gives me her name and phone number, so I can text her about the club. I text her about the club while I'm still walking with her, so I know the number went through. I kick myself shortly after for not having her text me, and I do not come up with a text that even prompts a reply. I realize, there is a high chance I'll have to double text if I leave her side.

I ask why she's in Vegas. She is there for a Jewish convention.

I say, "Interesting. I've never heard of one of those. What happens at a Jewish convention?"

Vanessa responds, "I think it's just an excuse for Jewish people to hook up."

I say, "That's a good assumption."

Vanessa says, "Isn't that why everyone comes to Vegas?"

Probably the best response I can hear... I take this as an indicator that she wants to get laid.

I nod and say, "Sounds about right."

Vanessa goes into a rant at this point. She tells me she doesn't like Jewish guys. She likes Asians... jacked Asians specifically. It's one of the rare times I hear a disqualifier thrown the other way. I am bummed she beat me to it. Any disqualifier I say now will have less impact since she already said one. I do not acknowledge that statement and continue with letting her invest.

She asks if there are any dancing auditions right now in Vegas for gogo.

I say, "No." It's an odd question that she asked though because I have heard strippers tell me before that they were go-go dancers. It's a sort of defense mechanism that girls seem to use to gauge the people they are talking to. From what I have seen, go-go dancers say they are dancers, strippers say they are go-go dancers, and hookers say they are strippers, escorts, or private dancers.

I ask if she's also looking to dance for a strip club. I realize that talking about strip clubs could start a sexual thread, and I can demonstrate I am not judgmental. Also, there is a high chance that she has not told a lot of people about her wanting to be a stripper, so if that is her situation, I can get a lot of investment by going down that conversational path. At the same time, if she says "no," I know that is not a good conversational topic without losing anything.

She says, "No."

I am not convinced by her answer, I am curious about the truth, and the thread is an interesting one to talk about, so I follow up. I say, "Too bad. Some of my good friends are strippers. They make really good money doing it. It amazes me when I meet people who judge strippers. I think, it's a great profession. Here, girls can make more as a stripper than they will with an Masters degree, but some people are really close-minded. Anyhow, where are you going right now?"

That statement primed the conversation. At least, she knows where I stand, so she knows I am open-minded and will not judge her. I also demonstrated preselection when I mentioned my stripper friends. I asked the question about where she is going to give her an out if she really does not want to talk about stripping, and learn the rest of her logistics to develop a plan for this set.

Vanessa tells me she is staying at the Tropicana with her pregnant sister and is going to the room to eat the food Vanessa just bought and is carrying because she has not eaten all day. I hesitate with what to do. Game-wise, I know I am supposed to stay in set. Work-wise, I have not done much so far today, and I will get a lot of shit from my boss if I do not get a lot of people into the club tonight. I am wondering if I should stay in set or go back to work.

Against every bit of game thinking, I decide to get back to work and tell her I'm going to get a drink in an hour, and she should come with me. Vanessa asks where. I hesitate and try to think of where would be logistically favorable.

I say, "Excalibur" because I want her buy-in, and I am

unsure if she will agree to a hotel that is further away even though logistically it will be favorable to me bringing her back to my place. She agrees. I say I will call her when I get off.

I take off after that and head back to promoting. I already texted her the info about the night club, so I don't text her any other text after I leave her side and decide I'll call her at 6pm when I get off because then I am not double texting, and I can iron out any logistical changes that I want to make to the game plan.

The next hour, all I am doing is kicking myself for not staying in set. Sure, work matters, but Vanessa was hot. Plus, things change fast on vacation. Plans may come up that interfere with things. I have decided the plan will be to have a drink at the bar in Excalibur then bounce to Flamingo if things are just going ok or pull directly to the place if things are going great. Then, I decide I can do even better. I can try to talk her into going to the Flamingo instead, so we are en route to the sex location when we meet. If the conversation does not go amazingly, we will do Excalibur as planned.

After work, I call her. She is working out at the Tropicana. I ask when she will be done. She says in 20 minutes. I say let's get a drink at Flamingo, and I say the Habitat in the back is gorgeous and she will love it (it's my best logistics in my opinion). She asks if we can meet and walk there. I tell her I'll pick her up at 6:45pm. She is cool with this. Great news for me. The car will make the pull to the place easy (plus, I have the car as a sex location).

I show up at Tropicana at 6:45pm, she is outside and gets in the car. We take Las Vegas Blvd to Flamingo because I feel the main boulevard will spike her BT since she has not been to Vegas before, and I think that a side street will hurt comfort since she is not as familiar with the area and a side street may freak her out.

There is so much traffic on Las Vegas Blvd. It's nuts! It's going to take 45 minutes to go 2 blocks! I am annoyed but do not let her see that. She is already investing in me. Sure enough, she strips in her hometown Denver. She tells me she started stripping 2 months ago in Denver. She tells me she will never tell her parents. She talks about the stripper shoes that she likes to wear.

I'm not kino-ing in the car to reward. The center console is in the way, so any action I take will be very weird. She points out how slow traffic is. Now that she has noted it too, it's time to take an alternate route. I agree and turn on the next street Harmon and then take Koval the side street parallel to the strip to get to the Flamingo.

We park at Flamingo. I lead her to the back area of the Flamingo by holding her wrist and walking a half foot in front of her. The wrist hold turns into a handhold, and she is squeezing my hand as we walk. Turns out she LOVES flamingos. She looks at them for a few minutes.

While we are standing in the Habitat outside with the waterfall flowing and the BT high, I try to kiss Vanessa. She pulls away. She says kissing weirds her out and that she has never understood kissing. Vanessa follows that rejection with, "But I'm interested to see what other moves I have…"

I shrug. It's a weird blend of comments. I know reacting and talking about kino is not the right move, so I figure ignoring is the next best thing. I lead her behind the waterfall into the Employees Only area. From there, we climb up a backside of the waterfall, so we are on top, looking down on the rest of the exhibit. It's a cool view, and she is only the second girl I have climbed up here with.

She asks, "How many times have you done this before?"

It's an interesting set because she is suggestive and inquisitive but continues to go with everything. I am honest because I cannot think of any downside to saying I have done it once before (She will definitely know if I say it's the first time I have climbed on top of this waterfall). I say, "Only once."

We sit and she tells me, "I think this is where you are supposed to tell me stuff about you, so you get more attracted to me."

Again, it's an interesting statement from her. I'm not used to girls being this much into the game. The play-by-play is a unique spin on things. I decide to step things up a notch to see what will happen, "It seems like you know all of the steps, how about we just skip everything and go to my place?"

She pauses in thought and says, "Let's still go through the steps."

Then almost as if she caught herself, she says, "That doesn't mean anything is going to happen though."

I nod my head. Based on all of her investment and her indications that I do this a lot, I know comfort is the right move. She obviously thinks I'm a player, which means I have attraction. I show her pics of me as a kid and show her how I used to be heavy and tell her I also used to be socially awkward.

She says I am where she used to be. She says where I haven't figured myself out yet and am lost. I am concerned the conversation is not moving in the direction I want things to go because I want her to like me not mentor me. I ask her a little about her and who she used to be. That takes the conversation off of me and gets more investment to balance things out. I note not to sound super troubled in the future comfort talks because it triggers the wrong type of frame.

We are up above the waterfall about 30 minutes when Vanessa says she wants a drink. I say, "Yeah. Great idea. Me too. That actually reminds me. Check this out…"

I pull up the picture of the Skittles vodka that is on my phone. I say, "My friend just made this stuff. He mixed Skittles with Smirnoff. See how there is one bottle for each flavor? You can tell the different flavors because of the color of the vodka. It's supposed to taste just like Skittles. I really want to try it. Come to think of it. My place is like 5 minutes from here, and I wanted to show you a stand up comedy video from me performing that's on my laptop. Want to go there for a sec before I drop you off at Tropicana and try it?"

She agrees, and we head to the house. On the drive, I point out a few things about Vegas, saying that we are a normal town like everywhere else because she was asking a few questions of what living in Vegas was like earlier. I figure, pointing out different things about the city off the strip will distract her from thinking about leaving the strip with someone that she does not know too well and build comfort because I am reminding her how this city is like any other, so she has no need to be anxious about being off the strip while in Vegas. She is very interested when I point out the college and no mention of how far off the strip we are going.

When we get to the house, she is amazed at the size of the house and wants a tour. A full house tour is a bad idea. It will take away from the mystique, so I decide I will give her a selective tour that helps with the set. But first, I pour her a drink with the Skittles vodka. She picks the flavor she wants to try. I fill to glasses with ice and then pour the

Skittles vodka.

We walk into the backyard. I show her the pool and the coy pond. We hang out by the hot tub for a second and talk. I have not kissed her yet, which is throwing off my game. I figure I need deeper investment. It's too cold outside though. She is shivering. I am too. I tell her we should go inside. She follows.

Vanessa asks me to see the rest of the house. I bring her into the spare room since mine has bunkbeds in it, and one of my roommates is sleeping. She is surprised at how bare the room is. It freaks her out. I think up a justification quickly, so she does not think I'm a crazy person with bare white walls (The room definitely looks like a room that you would expect to see someone in a straight jacket in). I tell her I just moved into the room from another room and all of my stuff was still in the other room. That calms her down. She says I need to put posters up or something. I make a mental note that in the future, I will mention the white walls to take the pressure off before going into the room.

I'm confused how to escalate without any making out, but she has been cool with coming back to the place, she has been in set for a decent amount of time, and we are now in the sex location, so... I decided to skip the kissing step and escalate as though that already happened. I start my revised escalation process by kissing her neck. Next, I move my mouth up towards her ear and start kissing and lightly licking the earlobe. I rub her breast from outside her shirt (she's not wearing a bra), then I run my hands down her pants and am touching her inner thighs.

She mentions something about the hot tub. Sounds like she wants to do something other than escalation. I know that the hot tub is not a bad play, but it also takes me out of the sex location. That means, I will be going backwards in set. Also, the hot tub will take 30 minutes to heat up. That means, there is a gap of time that I will have to fill doing something likely outside of the sex location with her. I try to come up with a solution that will meet what the hot tub can offer that is in the room now… The Shower!

I rationalize that the shower is close enough to the hot tub; there is water in both. I say "Let's go in the hot tub."

I lead her into the bathroom where the shower is, and I turn on the shower. Then I think that we will eventually need a towel, so I tell her I'll be back in a sec. I go out of the room for a second to get a towel.

When I come back into the room, Vanessa says she wants to go outside of the room and hang out and talk. I realize that leaving the room was a terrible idea, and obviously the shower plan did not work. It's clear she needs more comfort.

We go to the couch in the main room. I grab the photos I have from the closet that I have used to build comfort in other sets. The next 45 minutes entails us sitting on the couch and her asking me to tell her more about my life. Fifteen minutes in, I am struggling immensely. I show her a picture of my dog and tell her how my dog got put down. I show pictures of me in the woods, of me as a kid. I show her my stand up comedy routine from online. No matter what I show her or tell her, Vanessa always says, "Tell me more."

I'm grasping at straws. I don't know what more I need to say to build comfort. I also have <u>Californication</u> playing on the TV. I felt that was the best thing to have in the background to hopefully help with keeping her interested in sex.

I run out of things to talk about. Max comes into the

main room at one point to see how I'm doing. It's pretty clear I feel out of my element. Finally, I run out of things to tell Vanessa about. I feel like I have told her every vulnerable story that exists. I try something new.

I lead her over to the arcade-style skateboard game we have in our house. I figure, "Maybe it's not comfort any more. Maybe, it's BT."

I tell her to play. The game is a lot of fun. There is a skateboard that you stand on while playing that makes the whole game really interactive. She does terribly on her own. Wipe out after wipe out. I get on after she bombs, and I do a lot better.

Then, I decide I will have us both play at the same time. That means, we both get on the skateboard at the same time. I get on first. Then, I help her get on. It's great. Her ass is right in my crotch, and the rest of her body is basically right on top of mine. This is great. We do terribly on the game, but the whole time, we are playing our hips are moving in sync. It's insanely sexual. I'm basically thrusting her every time we do a jump or turn.

After the game is over, I start kissing the back of her neck. She is a little more responsive than last time. No sense stopping and leading her to the room when we have a good thing going… Bringing her to the room before she is fully aroused will only trigger more LMR, so I know not to bring her to the room a second time until she is fully on board with sex. I put my hands down her pants. She is still standing with her ass in my crotch, so my hands going down her pants is about as easy as putting my hands in my pockets. She lets me start to massage her thighs then whispers that we should not do anything sexual with Max right by us.

I grab her by the hand and lead her to the spare room.

Once inside, her clothes come off instantly. She is just in her panties. I take off my shirt, then tell her to take off my pants. I want more buy-in from her because she has been so passive this whole time. If I am going to hit resistance, I would rather hit it now and handle it before moving to the next step where we are both naked.

She says, "Wait. I want a massage first."

She lies face down on the bed. I foresee the massage quickly turning into sex, and I quickly fish a condom from my pants pocket and slip it under the pillow on the bed in case my pants come off at some point during the massage. I start to massage her lower back, and I am doing an appalling job; I am terrible with massages. I start massaging her ass. She loves her ass being massaged she tells me (and I love squeezing it). I start massaging lower on her ass toward where her pussy is to help stimulate blood flow there and to possibly start fingering her from behind. I am going slowly. Every part of this escalation process feels fragile, like it will fall apart with any misstep.

My pants are still on. She tells me she wants to give me a dance. Sounds like a step in the right direction... I lie on the bed, and she straddles me. As the dancing is going on, I pull off my pants and boxers at the same time. She says we're not going to have sex. I say, "Ok. It's more comfortable like this is all."

She lets the pants come off. I assume she needs more arousal. While she straddles me, I start fingering her. She tells me to rub her clit. I start to rub her clit with my fingers. As she gets more and more aroused, I transition to rubbing my dick against her clit and slit. This goes on for 5-10 minutes. She is turned on, but I still have not put on a condom... I take the chance...

I whisper, "I want to stick my dick in you."

Vanessa moans, "Do you have a condom?"

I grab the condom from by the pillow and put it on my dick in a smooth and quick motion (as quickly as I can without her thinking I'm moving too fast). Then, I stick my dick in. Grinding turns into missionary. Missionary turns into doggie, and doggie with Vanessa is amazing. Her ass combined with the tightness of her whole tiny body, combined with the feeling of complete calm after finally penetrating puts me over the edge. I cum. Hard. She isn't done yet... She wants to keep going.

I quickly go to the bathroom, wash my dick off, and throw on another condom. She's on all fours with her ass in the air, ready to be fucked again. Don't think I can ask for a better site... We go for a while before I finally go limp. Girl is insatiable.

I drop her off at her place later that night. She is all giggly and thanks me for the fun time and drinks. The next day, she checks out the pool party I put her on the guestlist for.

HARRIET

I am at 1Oak with Max. It's early in the night, and I see a girl named Bella that is just Max's type that is checking out his Mohawk. It's a clear indicator of interest. If I open Bella for Max, he can get in set without showing any interest. Me opening his set and introducing him gives him will give Max an easier time to build attraction with Bella; introduction is like the ultimate indirect. I open Bella, transition, then introduce Max the first opportunity I see for a smooth introduction.

I start talking to one of her friends to occupy the potential obstacle and learn logistics. I find out there are 5 girls total in the group; only 4 are at the club. One of the five is already back at Excalibur because she got kicked out of 1Oak. That fact let's me know 2 things: 1) The girls are all about partying, and 2) their room at Excalibur is a bad sex location.

Harriet is making out with some guy who bought them drinks the night before. The girl I am talking to freaks out, which lets me know she is the Mother Hen of the group. The Mother Hen says that Harriet has a boyfriend. The Mother Hen tells me that all the girls in the group (aside from Bella) are in relationships. The Mother Hen finishes her statement with, "…and I am married. There's no girls here for you, so you can go."

I choose to stay, not knowing whether Max will need me in this set for the long haul; I know for the moment Max needs me… I can already see the Mother Hen eying Max up and down. If I peel off, the Mother Hen will immediately swoop in and knock Max out of set, even though Bella is clearly enjoying his company. I tell the Mother Hen, "I completely agree. No one is getting laid tonight!"

With the energy of the club and everything going on, I know the Mother Hen hears what I just said, but I don't think she registers how odd of a statement I just made. I ask the Mother Hen to introduce me to her friends now that she is disarmed. The Mother Hen introduces me to one girl who looks tired and Harriet who was just making out with the other guy.

I text Max the rest of the girls are taken and that he needs to isolate his girl quickly if he wants his set to stay together. Meanwhile, the girls are distracted by a performance on stage. The distraction on stage gives Max an opportunity to move with Bella somewhere else in the club that is out of sight of the group of girls. Before fully out of sight, the Mother Hen starts looking around. I can tell she is searching, and I want Max to get in the clear. I point out the confetti to the Mother Hen while laughing. It's a silly distraction, but the distraction works and Max and Bella are hidden somewhere else in the club.

The Mother Hen and tired girl in the group decide to leave and do not make another mention of Max and Bella. I figure "out of sight, out of mind" and know not to bring up another mention of things to them.

Now, there are two girls left: Bella and Harriet. Max is in isolation with Bella. Harriet asks where Bella and Max are. I say, "I was wondering the same thing. We should go look for them."

I know Harriet will go looking for Max and Bella with or without me. I know that if I am on board, I can buy Max more time in isolation if more time in isolation is good for the set as a whole. I lead Harriet away from where I saw Max lead Bella. I am maximizing his time in isolation before we will bump into him and Bella.

Halfway into the search, Harriet is getting annoyed with me for not bringing her to Bella. Harriet says that Bella and Harriet lost each other a night ago and that Harriet doesn't want the two to be separated again tonight. This is also good news to me. A group that is willing to separate is a group that is more willing to go to the sex location of two guys they just met instead of going to the Excalibur...

I weigh the pros and cons of keeping the two separated from each other. I decide that Harriet is on the hunt and will find Bella one way or the other. If Harriet finds Bella later, Harriet will blame Max for keeping Bella away from her. Harriet will definitely not let Max leave with Bella. On the other hand if I lead Harriet to Bella, I will get the credit for finding her friend, which will build rapport with the group and give her comfort in knowing that if she and Bella are separated again, Harriet can count on me to find them. I choose the second option.

I lead Harriet to Max and Bella for the long-term play. The girls talk. Max and I speak. He is doing great on investment. Bella's brother passed away a few days ago... She is emotional and with great loss and sadness usually comes extreme horniness. Max has already kissed her and seeded the Jolly Rancher vodka at the house. I tell him about the girls' logistics, so he knows our place is best for the sex location.

After the girls talk, Bella comes back to Max. Max and Bella go to the bathroom. Harriet and I stay behind. Harriet is telling me that she is the wild one. I can see how wild Harriet is being while most guys will be thrilled by Harriet's forwardness with touching, the girl who says she is the wild one usually is not. Usually the self-proclaimed "wild one" is the validation set. I have already seen her hook up with a guy that financed her drinks the other night who is no longer around, so I suspect she loves to let guys think she is sexual but rarely goes as far as she alludes to. Also, the Mother Hen said Harriet had a boyfriend, which adds to the likelihood that Harriet wants validation more than a hook up. A validation set knows she can get sex whenever she wants but often misses the attention she gets from guys because most guys ignore her the second she mentions she has a boyfriend. I test Harriet to see if she is all talk or if she really is "wild."

I ask, "What is the wildest thing that you have done in Vegas?"

She says, "Oh sorry. I have a boyfriend."

I am taken off guard. Girls only bring up disqualifiers when they sense a guy is showing them interest. I feel like I have not been showing her much interest so far, so that is an odd statement...

Now if she is going to whip out the boyfriend card before I have shown my interest, it means she wants me to be interested in her. And if she is going to disqualify me to build attraction and play the validation card, you had better believe I am going to have her put her money where her mouth is...

I kiss Harriet on the lips.

She kisses back. At the same time there is a look of shock on her face. It's clear she is confused… I'm guessing guys don't usually escalate in response to a disqualifier… I decide to disqualify back (and hence the circus begins).

When the kiss breaks, I say, "I'm gay."

She says, "Really?"

I cannot believe she actually asked that. I respond sarcastically and amused, "Oh yeah, I'm super gay."

She asks, "Are you serious?"

I cannot believe she asked that follow up question. I try to imagine a gay guy EVER describing himself as "super gay." Sounds incredibly unlikely. I say, "Oh totally, so serious."

She says, "Oh ok. Great!"

Words cannot describe how amazed I am that she just believed me… Then, I look down and realize I'm wearing a super tight blazer, tailored at least a size too small (my super tight bright red pants are not helping the cause that I look straight either). Her willingness to believe I am gay may be ridiculous, but I can see where she is coming from. Then, I think, "Shit. Let's see what happens when I play the gay card."

I immediately text Max that I am going to pretend to be gay the rest of the set. He thinks it's hilarious.

The next 45 minutes is absolute ridiculousness. I act as stereotypically gay as possible, and Harriet follows my lead. She is loving every minute of it, and I am completely distracting from Max and Bella. I take Harriet onto the dance floor. I am being so much more sexually suggestive. My dance moves consist of air humping, grinding, me walking up to her sexually then lightly pushing her away when we get close. We keep getting close to kissing, but I always turn away. She is rubbing up and down my body.

She even rubs my belly like I'm Buddha at one point. I keep telling her that we are the hottest people on the dance floor in the most vain way I possibly can, and she keeps agreeing and says I am the hottest guy on the dance floor and all the other bitches are jealous that she has me instead of them. I am amazed how far I can push this card. I am beginning to think there is no breaking point.

I'm even pretending to scope out other guys while we are dancing. She is nodding encouragingly as we're dancing as though I should go and dance with these different guys. I always have a reason for why I will not dance with each guy. The reasons include, "He's a bad dancer," "He's a bad dresser," "He smells," "Not a nice enough ass." Harriet is nodding enthusiastically at how picky I am while I'm surprised she still thinks I'm gay.

I know all of this sexual dancing and pulling off is doing the job when Harriet says, "I so want to make out with you."

I laugh and say, "I would need another drink before I could even consider that…"

Perfect segue to the bar. Harriet and I go over to the bar. She buys me a drink. I'm tired of dancing and only have so many "gay moves" in me. I make a mental note that I can blame the alcohol later as an excuse for escalating on her. I have heard of gay guys making out with chicks before, so I know I can at least get to the make out without any question from Harriet about my sexuality… I still cannot figure out how I will close though…

I ask more questions about Bella to see how I can help Max's set. Harriet cares about Bella having a good time and says that Bella has been having a rough couple of weeks and Vegas has not been too great yet, so they want a good night tonight. That's good news to me so long as I can make sure Max and Bella get isolation in a sex location.

Max and I bump into each other at the bar. Right when I see him, I greet him with the most flamboyant "Hi" he's ever seen me do and then I say Hi to Bella who I have not actually met yet. Max is cracking up with my demeanor. I compliment Bella on what she is wearing. Harriet sees that I am trying to have Bella have a better night and says, "Isn't he great? You know he's gay?"

That's too much for Max, he says, "Oh my gosh! He's so gay!"

I then do the stereotypical gay hand gesture, and then Bella says, "Oh my gosh! He's great! And he's so gay!"

The girls check in with each other which gives Max and I a second to talk and compare notes with the set. He is doing well. As long as we can have Harriet on board with coming back to the place, we are good. I say we can do that. Max also says that I might be able to fuck Harriet if I give her LMR.

I think about it and realize he is right. It's the best strategy I can think of to take me past make out. We agree we will pull within the next 30 minutes and go back into our own sets. I grab Harriet by the wrist and announce in front of Max and Bella, "Let's go girl. None of those sluts on the dance floor are even close to as hot as we are!"

That sets Harriet off. She loves the validation. She says to Bella before we get on the dance floor again, "I love him! He's SO GAY!!"

Harriet and I are back on the dance floor. I now have one more drink in me, so I have plausible deniability to kiss her. While we are doing our sexual dance back and forth, I let her kiss me. It turns into a full tongue-down-my-throat make out. I pull away after a few seconds and wipe my lips like there is something nasty on them. Then I say, "That was hot, but let's get another drink…"

With Harriet's BT up, I know this is the best time to pull. I lead her by the wrist back to where Harriet and I left Bella and Max just a few minutes ago. I say, "Hey. Let's go get a drink outside. It's so hot in here!"

The whole group heads outside the club. Harriet says she wants to play roulette. We head to the roulette table. On the way over, I give her a devious look. I decide that the best pull for Max with his girl is by getting Harriet on board with us. While Harriet does not expect us to hook up, I have a good feeling she would like nothing more than to help her friend get laid if she thinks it's her idea…

I say, "Hey. I've got a fun idea…"

She says, "Yeah, what?"

I say, "Well, Max and Bella obviously like each other. What if we helped them hook up?"

She says, "That sounds like fun!"

I say, "We're like matchmakers! We're such a hot team! No one can touch this shit!"

She gets all excited when I say that. She loves when I validate how hot she and I are. She talks about how we are such great wingmen.

We get to the roulette table, and Harriet loses all of her money in 2 spins. Fine by me. I say, "Forget this! Let's go drink the Jolly Rancher vodka!"

On cue, Harriet says that sounds like fun, and Matt says it sounds good. Bella gets on board with the band wagon. We walk to the parking lot, and I drive. The girls continue to repeat how gay I am, and I spew absolute nonsense that no real gay guy would say, amazed they still think I am gay.

The girls do get a little nervous on the drive to the place. They comment on how the neighborhood off the strip is a little sketchy. My flamboyance and Max's BT spikes help to ease that uncertainty.

Once we get to the place, everything calms down. The girls are impressed with the size of the house. I tell them we got the house on foreclosure because I have hit the problem before where girls start asking questions about money and how we can afford such a place. Saying we got it on foreclosure shuts those questions up before they start. We all do a shot of Jolly Rancher Vodka then Harriet and I stay by the bar while Max brings Bella to the backyard. I know the plan will be for him to bring her back in through the other door that connects the backyard to his room. There is a security sensor on that other door that will make a beeping noise when he goes through. That will be my cue that he is in his bedroom with Bella. When Max is in the sex location with Bella, I will see if I can close Harriet.

Meanwhile, Harriet and I talk about how great of wingmen we are for Max and Bella. I agree. I repeat how hot we were at the club and how all the other bitches were so jealous. Agrees and says all the bitches were jealous of her for being with me. The sensor beeps. I know Max is bringing her into his room, so coast is clear for me to try escalating.

I tell Harriet we should cuddle and lead her to a vacant room upstairs. She is fine with cuddling. She makes some suggestion about possibly doing more, and I brush it off. I know I need to play hard to get for this to work.

We get into the room. I close the door, and I lay on top of the blankets while she goes below. She says she wants me under the blankets. I say, Ok. Then, I take my pants off, saying I will be more comfortable. We are spooning, and I am beginning to get hard. There is a chick wearing close to nothing in my bed... The gig is up. I am hard.

She is confused with why my dick is a little hard. I say, "I don't know. This doesn't happen. I'm gay. Maybe it's the booze."

Harriet says she is a nurse and will inspect my penis. I cannot complain about how she wants to solve this problem. She sits up, and pulls down my boxers and starts to squeeze my penis. She tells me I have a pretty penis then puts it back in my boxers and mentions her boyfriend.

Harriet keeps saying it is be ok if we kiss while we're laying down. I act indecisive about kissing. We kiss then I quickly pull away. I wait a minute and try again and do the same thing. On the third time, I kiss and turn it into a make out. I decide to pretend my animalistic urges are taking over against my desire to only sleep with men. I roll on top of her and start grinding my pelvis against her, while kissing her neck and lightly biting up and down her neck to her ear lobe. She starts biting my neck.

I tell her, "This is amazing. I haven't gotten this excited about a girl in a really long time. I don't know what is happening."

I say that because I can obviously not control my dick any more and because I figure if she realizes that I have had sex with girls before, I do not hit the potential issue of her being afraid of fucking me because she does not want to pop my straight cherry, so to speak. I remember seeing a gay guy tell a girl in a movie once that he had slept with girls in the past, which is what inspired the idea.

I also tell her that the one thing I miss about girls is that girls like to have foreplay and teasing. That way, I figure I have some more plausible deniability of why I am escalating so much if I truly do not like girls. I let her think I enjoy the act of foreplay more than whether it is with a man or a women. I now have the excuse after the fact that "all I wanted was some intense petting and teasing…" and then say, "...but one things led to another and..."

She is writhing beneath me, loving that she has gotten me so turned on that I cannot help myself.

Then I whisper into her ear, "I think, I want to be inside of you."

She asks, "Are you sure?"

(Btw, I mentioned to her earlier that I've been with girls before but it's just been awhile. I didn't want her to have any moral grounds against fucking me based on her being my first or something)

I say, "Yes."

She asks, "Do you have a condom?"

I've already placed a condom on the bed as I was taking my pants off. I pull it out. She helps me put it on. I am on top of her, and she holds my dick by the shaft, looking me in the eyes as she guides my dick inside her vagina.

Now, we are fucking. As I fuck her, I keep saying how good it feels and how crazy this whole night has been. And then I say in surprise that I think I might actually cum. That gets Harriet worked up. She says, "Yes. Cum for me. Cum."

I cum and make an orgasm that is more vocal than normal to validate her that I came. After a few minutes, I look her in the eyes and tell her I can't believe that just happened.

To my amazement, Harriet consoles me, she says, "It's ok. You couldn't help yourself. You are still gay. It's ok to be sexually confused."

I go in the bathroom to wash my dick off, and Harriet says, "I can't believe what just happened. I actually got you to have sex with me, and you're so gay."

I do not even know how to respond to what I am hearing. We cuddle. She is big spoon while she continues to build comfort with me. We talk about what just happened, and I say how I did not expect any of this. She says we can go again if I want. I pretend to have to think about it. I pause for 45 seconds, and then say, "Okay."

I leave the room to get a condom and listen in on Max and how he is doing. I cannot tell from listening if he has closed yet. I go back upstairs into the room Harriet is in. I tell her I want her on top because I never get to just look at the girl and appreciate her beauty. We go for awhile, til we fall off the bed, then I fuck her doggie til I cum again. Harriet is so happy that she is making me cum.

As we lay there after the second round, Harriet tells me, "It isn't cheating because you are gay... I knew you were gay the second I met you."

I just lay there and listen to the worst justification I think I have ever heard for why a girl cheated on her boyfriend, and I cross my fingers Max got laid too.

The next morning, Max and I drive the girls back to Excalibur. Harriet asks me to friend her on Facebook. I do. I also remove the info that I like women from my profile, at least until these girls leave Vegas. Harriet tells me as I'm hugging her goodbye at Excalibur that she has the perfect guy for me in Canada and that he's super hot. I roll my eyes on the inside and thank her.

EMMA

I see Emma a cute blonde talking to a taller girl at the patio at Tryst. I open Emma by asking if she is wearing a sailor jacket.

She tells me that she is wearing jumper, a dress that has a British style. Emma's accent clues me in that she is British, and I disqualify her for being from Britain, saying it would never work out between us.

Emma has a good reaction to my open by turning fully toward me and being engaged immediately. She has an even better reaction after my break in rapport. She laughs and continues to watch me as if she's waiting in anticipation for whatever the next thing is that I am going to say. It's so tempting to break rapport again since she is enjoying my company, but I know that I have enough attraction for the moment. I have to elicit investment and learn logistics.

I ask who Emma is there with, and Emma points out her tall friend Sophie. Emma has been friends with Sophie for a long time she says. That's good to know. It means, the girls probably do not have a problem with Same Night Lays around each other, so Max and I should have a fairly easy time bringing them back to the place as long as neither he nor I does anything stupid.

Max talks to Sophie before I have a chance to introduce him. I lock in against the wall that Emma was initially leaning on, so she is turned toward me and slightly away from Max and Sophie. Max locks in near the doorway with Sophie turned towards him. We have mini-isolation.

There is not much more to the time at the club after this. She smokes a few cigarettes and gives me them to smoke with her when I ask for the cigarettes. I do not care to smoke, but smoking will build another commonality and build a little rapport between me and Emma.

It is about 45 minutes to an hour of my qualifying Emma. I could tell on the open that she liked me, but I am not sure how much she likes me. I want to solidify the attraction with the kiss, but that seems so quick. I imagine the possibility that Emma will react surprised to the kiss and grab Sophie's attention to have the two leave set. If Max has not built enough attraction with Sophie yet, a bad reaction from Emma could trigger that. I decide to wait for a more clear signal from Emma that she likes me.

That signal never comes through body language. Ever since open, Emma has not been showing me increased interest. She always remains about 8 inches away from me. Sure, it's close but not "let's fuck" close. Emma is investing, and this is one of those nights where I feel like I am asking question after question in like an interview mode. The investment stays mostly at low-level and occasionally I dig deeper into mid-level investment. The one nice things she says is that she is "very single." I take her telling me that as a solid IOI and wonder why she is not going deeper if she likes me already.

I am confused with how her initial interest and her statement about being "very single" do not fully mesh with her not showing more interest in body language and her investment that is not super deep. I zone out a few times while she is talking to mentally break down the whole set and figure out if I am on track; I miss a few things she says and ask a question that she had just said the answer to. She looks at me as though I have not been paying attention, and I luckily save myself by saying, "I mean, I know you said that. What I meant was…" and asking a question that was more in depth. I am lucky she overlooks those small details.

While I am breaking down the set, I realize why I am having so much trouble… I have not been physical in this set! Emma is the second girl I opened tonight, so I have not hit my stride with my game for the night. Now that I am thinking about it, I have hardly escalated at all so far in this set. I may have touched her upper arm on open and possibly shaken her hand. It's annoying to have to introduce kino into set rather than do it on open; the kino seems less consistent and less natural because I have not been doing it so far. I know I need to start with small steps and work up from there, so I look for opportunities to reward her investment with high fives and first bumps to get things moving.

Sophie wants a drink, so Max announces that we are all going to get drinks. He grabs Sophie by the wrist and leads her through the club to the bar near the stripper pole at Tryst. The place is an absolute mess. It is always so congested inside. If I were not leading Emma by the wrist, there is no chance she could have stayed with us. I am doing all I can to continue walking tall while forcing my way through the sea of people. I make sure to keep a smile on my face, so I do not look annoyed with getting tripped every other step and body checked by the drunks walking in the opposite direction.

When we get to the bar, Max and I go up to the bar with the girls and take a step back once they are locked in. This stops us from falling into the awkward situation where the girls expect us to pay for their drinks. We do not want to fall into the provider frame and be like every other guy who has bought drinks at the club for them before.

Max and I debrief about how things are going. Max says his girl likes him, and he has kissed her. I say I am pretty sure mine likes me but screwed up escalation so far. Max says he already seeded the Jolly Rancher vodka. We decide we will pull after the girls have their drink.

Sophie turns back to Max and hands him a drink. Emma hands me one. We thank the girls for buying our drinks and lead the girls back to the patio. The patio is actually farther from the exit than the bar, but there is no other good place to stand and talk inside Tryst with these girls without getting bumped a ton, so we go back to the patio to have the drink.

I tell Emma that the drink reminds me of the Jolly Rancher vodka that we have at our place. I say that our friend just made it, and we have not even tried it yet. I say I cannot wait to try it later. I ask which flavor she thinks she will like the best to build more buy-in for the pull that is going to happen soon.

We talk for another 10-15 minutes. Max and I are locked in with Sophie turned towards Max and Emma turned towards me. Occasionally, Max and I talk with each other to promote a slightly more group conversation since we are about to bounce as a group. The conversation is all low level at this point; it is the wrong time to go deep since we are about to bounce. If I need to go deep, I will do it at the place. I still have not kissed Emma. Since Max is leading the pull and already kissed Sophie, I do not have to kiss

Emma. A kiss with the pull so close would also put a lot of pressure on the pull for Emma because it would feel like the kiss is the reason I am going for the pull rather than incidental, which removes plausible deniability as an excuse the next day.

Max says we should do shots of the Jolly Rancher vodka. I say that is a great idea, and we lead the girls out of the club. The car ride back is very light and playful lots of small teases about how the US is better than England and vice versa. The girls are laughing.

At the place, the whole group does a shot at the bar. I lead Emma to the backyard to smoke a cigarette, knowing that the backyard is good for isolation with me and Emma since I do not need a sex location yet. I also know that Sophie will have an easier time sneaking off into Max's room when Emma is not watching. Even though the girls are close friends and Emma probably would not mind Max and Sophie hooking up, giving Max and Sophie a little privacy is the safe play. Max leads Sophie in the direction of his room.

Emma and I are alone outside sitting on the couch and smoking a cigarette. It's time to make a move if I am going to. The outside is great because it's darker than inside, which creates a more seductive atmosphere. The cushions on the couch sink down deep, so the arms of the couch give an added feeling of seclusion from the rest of the outside. The only thing between us and a make out is the cigarettes and me taking action.

I think it will be awkward going for a kiss while Emma and I are smoking because our breath will be bad, and I may accidentally get burned by the cigarette butt. If I do not do it now though, Emma may get up to go back inside after the cigarette since it is cold and the reason for going outside in the first place was to smoke. Going inside to a well-lit room is moving backwards in set. It's now or never.

I lean in toward Emma to kiss her. Emma is sitting about a foot away from me, and we are both facing the same way, so I basically have to turn my whole body to get in a position for our lips to touch. I have my cigarette in my hand that is away from her, so I do not accidentally burn her and cause a state break. There is nothing subtle or sexy about my move. I make a note to kiss earlier in the future, so there are not awkward moments like this again.

Sophie kisses back. She puts her cigarette in the ash tray and grabs my arms and pulls herself onto me. I make sure my cigarette hand stays far away. Her hands are rubbing through my hair as we make out. "I guess she likes me after all," I think to myself.

The make out is everything I want it to be except it is too much. I need to keep the sexual tension in the set. I gently push her off me smiling and say, "One sec. Let's finish our cigarettes."

The cigarette is more of a formality than anything else. I would rather fuck than smoke, but I wanted a small justification to stop the make out. It sucks to stop her from doing something I like and have been wanting her to do all night, but there is a glass ceiling if I let the escalation continue out here. It only takes a pang of cold or a noise over the neighbors fence to trigger LMR…

I grab Emma by the wrist and lead her to the upper room. We are making out immediately. She is just as hot and heavy as before. Then, she stops.

Emma looks up at me nervously, "I can't do anymore right now…"

I stay silent and continue to look at her. I have a feeling I know what she is about to say…

Emma says, "It's just that I'm coming off my period…"

I continue looking at her. I know she is nervous I am going to be grossed out. I smile and say, "That's okay. I don't mind."

And we're back on!

We go onto the futon in the corner of the bare room. We are making out more. Emma is undressing me. I am rubbing her pussy from above her clothing. I am partially fingering her through her panties and jumper. I tell her I can feel how wet she is and it is turning me on. She grabs my cock and starts stroking it.

This is my first time dealing with a jumper, and I am not thrilled. The thing is a pain in the ass to take off. So annoying to have a wardrobe situation when she and I are in the heat of the moment. I am on top straddling her in my boxers, socks and unbuttoned shirt while she is stroking my dick. I am trying to take off the jumper gracefully, but the damn thing will not come off. I would prefer not to tear the clothing and risk a state break. After several minutes of getting no closer to removing the jumper, she tells me, "Just tear it off."

Done.

I tear off the top button. Emma help me pull the jumper down to her legs then kicks it off. I am fingering her. She is already squirming and moaning. Emma asks if I have a condom. I take it from the pillow I placed it under while my pants were coming off, and I put the condom on.

We fuck. Her tiny body makes the sex so much more fun! We can flip positions easy. I can fuck her standing up while she is wrapped around my waist. I am loving it.

After sex, we go outside for a smoke. Emma asks how old I am. I say 23. She says she's 34. She looks slightly surprised about the age difference but does not say anything else about it. I text Max that Emma and I fucked, so I am good to take off any time if he is done fucking Sophie. No response, so…

I lead Emma back upstairs. We fuck for over an hour. She cums 3 times. I cum twice. When Emma and I come out of the room and go downstairs, Max and Sophie are in the living room. Sophie is fixing her hair, and Max is in his PJs. Max only puts on his PJs after he closed, so it looks like good news all around. Sophie and Emma smile at each other and then talk about their plans the next day and realize how late it is. Max and I drive the girls back to their hotel.

SANDY

I get a late start to my night. It's around 1:30am when I'm going out, but better late than never. It's Mexican Independence Day, and the clubs are celebrating the theme. It's not the usual holiday I'm used to celebrating, like Halloween or New Years, so I am entertaining myself by opening sets as I walk toward the club entrance by saying, "Happy Mexican Independence Day" in Spanish.

It seems like a funny and odd open coming from a white boy, and I am curious to see how people will react. The girls either ignore the open, and I smile and transition; or they laugh and speak Spanish back to me. Then, I open Sandy...

Sandy is leaving XS by herself. She is on her phone and about 100 feet from the club when I open her, saying, "Happy Mexican Independence Day" in Spanish. She stops walking and looks up from her phone and says in a curt tone, "What did you say?"

I'm amused by this new reaction. I repeat myself.

Sandy looks pissed. She crosses her arms and leans back on one leg. She says, "Do I look Spanish to you?"

It is clear she is not Spanish, but I am confused why she

is so offended. I decide I want to game Sandy instead of going into the club. I transition just like always, "No. You actually seem pretty friendly... Where are you from?"

She has a look of confusion on her face. I get why. It's pretty clear she is not friendly, but ignoring her rejection is the best strategy I have. I figure a few breaks in rapport, and the whole set will turn around. I am curious to see what happens. She tells me she lives at LVCC.

I say, "Las Vegas Country Club? No way! I used to live there! Now, you and I are definitely not going to get along."

I am excited she is at LVCC because it's only a few minutes from where we are at, which makes it a decent option for a sex location. I know mentioning I used to live there will build a little rapport and the disqualifier will break rapport.

That disqualifier sets Sandy off. She calls me smug and makes fun of my sweater and shirt combo (she is not doing the best job, but I commend her effort). She talks about how I'm such a douche and makes a few other unflattering statements. I have definitely not done anything to deserve this; all the same, I nod while I throw in light teases and logistical qualifiers to learn her logistics for the night. While I do not know what to do with her fury to me, I can see she is already investing a lot emotionally into this interaction, which is an indicator that I can turn this into sex.

It sounds like I opened her when she was on the way to meet the friend she came to XS with. Sandy and the friend decided they would meet at Eastside bar, just out of sight of where Sandy and I are standing presently. We have been standing in the hallway for 10-15 minutes now. Soon, she will start to feel the pain in her heels and want to sit. I would normally bring her to the closest bar or place to sit, but that brings me right to where Sandy will meet her friend. I lose isolation, and the friend may ruin everything.

Sandy has calmed down from the tirade. She has answered the other logistical questions (Her plan is to sleep tonight and work in the afternoon tomorrow), and now she is answering low level qualifiers, like where she works and how often she goes out. I suggest we get a drink at the Peppermill. Peppermill is about a block from XS and closer to LVCC, which moves the set toward the sex location. I also say that I came out to drink but have not had anything to drink yet and since XS is slowing down anyhow, Peppermill will be more fun. I make note to mention that I have not drank yet because I plan to drive to Peppermill in a few minutes, and I do not want Sandy to object that I may be drunk and hurt comfort. (I also think that I may be able to justify going to Sandy's place after Peppermill by saying that I want to keep drinking but not want to drive after, like I did in the set with the Paula).

Sandy agrees. She checks her phone. Sandy's friend has not messaged Sandy yet. I tell Sandy that we can come back if she needs to meet up with her friend.

As we are walking to the parking lot, I realize that things are moving quickly in set. If I want to keep the momentum, I should kiss Sandy now. I could lose all the tension on the trip to Peppermill, and I will have to start the whole cycle of breaking rapport all over again. It's possible we will not even have to go to the Peppermill if Sandy is ready to have sex now.

So, I kiss Sandy in the Wynn hallway outside of XS before we bounce to the Peppermill. Sandy kisses back. But she just kisses back. No start to a make out means Peppermill is the better move. There is also a look of surprise on her face, which confirms my decision to not skip steps. I think "Ok. She likes me but not enough to go to a sex location."

I open the door for Sandy, and she calls me a gentleman. That's a big shift in descriptors compared to what she was calling me in the first 10 minutes of meeting...

The conversation to Peppermill is light. Sandy says she cannot drive because she got a DUI a few months ago. Sandy says that there was an accident. The accident is an addition that I have not heard in most DUI stories. I make a note to bring that up later in set because if there was an injury, the DUI accident may be a very emotionally-charged topic.

At Peppermill, we each order a drink. We talk a little about our interests. I find out we like the same TV shows and that she has everything OnDemand. Great news for me. I just found a good justification for the pull!

We talk more about the shows that she has on the DVR at her place right now. I give a 2 second kiss to cement that things are on. Then, I ask if Sandy wants to get out of there and go watch TV at her place. She is fine with that.

I drive us to LVCC. When we get to her place, we go upstairs. Sandy says she does not do this a lot. She says I'm the third guy in three years that's been to her place. I do not have anything to say to that; there is nothing to say. Sandy starts undressing when we are up in her room without me saying or doing anything. Although Sandy claims she does not do this a lot, her actions tell me she knows the game plan pretty well... No need to comment on that. Any comment I make will sound judgmental.

The escalation is very straightforward. I follow her lead with undressing and palm a condom as I take my pants off. I approach her. We make out. We go over to her bed while making out. I get on top. I feel how wet her pussy already is with my hands and this time forego the fingering process since she is already ready to go. I open the condom and unroll it on my dick then go inside her.

We fuck collectively for 2-3 hours over the next 8 hours. We fuck in all kinds of different positions. After the first round, I am about to get up to grab another condom from my pants that are on the floor. Sandy makes me stay on the bed. She has her own stash of condoms. She grabs one, skips back to the bed, jumps on the bed, opens the condom, puts the unrolled condom on the tip of my hard dick, and uses her mouth to unroll the condom down my dick. An impressive talent as far as I'm concerned.

She keeps yelling out my name, which is a turn on. I cum twice. She cums a hell of a lot more than me. Sandy says she wants to see me again. I say Bye and agree we'll see each other again.

A few hours after I leave, Sandy sends a text thanking me for everything.

CANDIS

I am walking through Caesars on the way to Pure when I see Candis sitting by herself at a slot machine, texting on her phone. The scene immediately gives me a glimpse into what is probably going on in her night. I am guessing she has lost her friends, is annoyed, and is still up for doing something because the night is early but probably does not want to do a club. (I cross my fingers that is the case because then I already have isolation, she is emotionally charged, and I will not have to deal with the club and it's distractions, which will make the set run more smoothly for me.)

I open Candis. The reaction to the open is nothing special. She says one or two words then keeps texting. I transition then break rapport regardless.

Candis is positioned in her seat so she is facing outward, away from any other decent place for me to lock in. There is no place for me to lock in that will not be uncomfortable to be at or awkward from her perspective for me to be at after a couple of minutes. So, I go to sit on the other side of Candis and turn Candis's chair, so she is faced towards me. The new seating position is also better because now

Candis has a view of me and a wall rather than a view of the whole casino area, so I see anyone new that may come into the set first.

There is a protest from Candis for about 30 seconds when I reposition her chair. I ignore her annoyance with me, and she settles into her new position. Suddenly, Candis says, "You have to look away. You have really pretty eyes."

I have brown eyes. I do not have pretty eyes. That is an IOI. I try to kiss her. She turns away. I have only been in set for 2 minutes, so the kiss is. I continue talking to her as if nothing has happened. In the next 20 minutes, I will be rejected by Candis 3 more times when I try to kiss her. On the fifth time, she kisses me. Because Candis says "You have to look away," I assume she has a reason she cannot kiss me. Either she has a boyfriend or she made an agreement with friends that she would not hook up with a guy or she had a bad experience with a guy recently and does not want to get hurt/embarrassed again. There is something else going on. I am not about to shed light on that though. There is no good that can come from doing that...

It is an amusing 20 minutes of talking. Every once in a while, Candis will tell me to stop looking at her because of my eyes, and I go for a kiss. And Candis also tells me to stop talking more than once. She never says go away, just to stop talking...

I ignore her the first few times and continue to ask Candis qualification questions, which she qualifies to. Candis tells me she loves political debates. I say I could beat her in a debate.

She says I could not win a debate against her.

I say I want a legit debate with a white board to write our points on and that I had one at my house. I am just ranting about the debate and how I will win. The funny this is that I know nothing of politics, but I know my blind passion and emotions will keep things moving no matter how political any discussion gets on her end.

Candis tells me to stop talking, so I type on the notepad in my phone "lets go have a debate" and show Candis the message.

Candis types back "when and where tell me I'm there."

I type "There's a white board at my house. You can come, but have to promise to not be mean to my fish :)" because I know the break in rapport at the end will lighten the pressure of her coming back to my place. She smiles and nods. I kiss her to solidify attraction.

I get up and walk toward the self park where my car is. On the way, Candis bumps into a guy friend. Their body language shows an interesting level of familiarity. I wonder how they know each other. I sit back and pretend to be on my phone. I am not sure who I am supposed to be in this interaction, so I decide to let things run their course as long as she is not with him for long. The guy says he can't find his phone and asks Candis to call it. That request causes Candis to look at her phone. Candis sees missed calls from her friends and roommates. These are all calls Candis did not notice while she was talking to me… Candis calls them. She finds out they are not at the casino anymore.

Then Candis's behavior to me changes. She says she needs to go home and asks how all this is happening. I say, "It's crazy, I wasn't even planning on going out and now here we are."

I realize Candis drove too, so I do not mention I have a car and ask Candis to drive me home. I can use the car ride home to help get things moving in the right direction again. Candis agrees when she realizes I live pretty close.

Whatever conversation she had with her friends and however she knows that guy really changed her state. Right before we get into the car, Candis says, "Fuck my life."

I say, "Whatever you wish."

I mean that to be a joke. That freaked Candis out a sec. She says, "What's that supposed to mean?"

I do not have an amazing answer, and she clearly took it the wrong way. I make a note not to break rapport when a girl is distressed. I also realize how stupid I am to break rapport right before the car ride. I say, "Nothing. It was stupid and supposed to be funny."

Candis calms down briefly at that point. The car ride back is Candis saying how crazy it is that all this happened and saying she has a complicated story. I do not want to go into the long complicated story on the car ride. Wrong time for that. I'll only go into that if I do not sense I have enough comfort. I just say, "That's fine" to acknowledge what she said and leave things at that.

I kiss Candis once more when we pull up to a stop light on the drive home to re-establish where we are at after the massive state break. She kisses back. It is still unclear what is going to happen when we get to the house. The agreement changed from us going in to have a debate to her dropping me off. I am going to have to pull a miracle out of my ass to make this work.

We get to the house. I say, "Hey. That reminds me. Let's have that debate."

She says she is not interested in a debate.

I say, "Right. What about the stand up comedy video? I want you to see it."

She says she is not interested.

It is interesting because she is frustrated with whatever is going on with her friends, and I am pretty sure she wants to be here with me, so I make a play: I turn off the ignition to her car. I say, "Listen. You have had a long night. You should come inside a few minutes to relax."

She nods in agreement. I take the keys out of the ignition. She follows me into the house.

Inside, I kiss her. She says she doesn't want me to kiss her. She says she thinks she should go. I sense she's reluctant to be here, but she can just leave if she wants to. I figure that she may not want to kiss in the main room because it is too public. I go into the spare room. There is somebody asleep in there. Candis sees the guy asleep too…

Candis asks who the guy in the room is. I say a friend from out of town and that I am letting him crash in my room for the night. I realize, I have no room to fuck her in…

I lead Candis to the couch in the main room. I turn on computer, which is on the coffee table in case I need it for the set. Candis is looking around as if she is trying to take everything in. Then, Candis asks where I grew up. I'm thrilled! She finally wants comfort from me! If I can build enough comfort, we will have sex. It is nice to know where I am at in set after all this craziness.

Candis says she almost never goes out and has work at 8:30am. It is currently 5:30am. I nod, showing that I understand her situation and have her lay down on the couch.

We're cuddling, and I tell Candis where I grew up. Then I ask her about her best memory as a kid. She tells me something about singing Christmas carols. Then, Candis tells me that her brothers are drug addicts and she doesn't have the same relationship with them anymore.

I escalate with kissing on the neck and position her underneath me on the couch. We're making out, and I run my right hand up her thigh but get resistance when she grabs my hand as I am moving my hand close to her vagina.

There is 10 more minutes of making out and grinding before I realize I will not get any further escalation until I build more comfort. I stay on top of her and say again how I didn't expect any part of this night to happen.

Candis said earlier about how she feels our energies have met before. I bring that up again. I am playing the Serendipity card hard. I say, "Even if nothing else happens, us meeting was supposed to happen."

I ask Candis who her favorite superhero is. She never gives me an answer, so I ask another question.

Meanwhile, I pull the blanket on the couch over us. I realize the blanket will provide a feeling of privacy even though we are in the most public spot in the house.

I escalate again with LOTS of kissing around the neck. She REALLY likes that. She's running her hands along my waist line. I tell we how hard she's making me and that I want her to feel it while I guide her hand to my crotch. She feels it only for a few seconds before pulling away. It is good she felt it. Pulling away is an indicator that she is turned on but not enough yet.

My right hand goes into her pussy. I feel a tampon inside. I have never dealt with a tampon before, but I know what to do in theory. I use my index finger and middle finger to try to fish it out. The tampon is more slippery to pull out than I expect, but I get it out and toss tampon on the couch.

I am fingering Candis. She is moaning. This goes on for 3-5 minutes Til I think she's getting close to cumming. I do not want her to cum before I am inside her. Her orgasm will release all of the sexual tension for her. So I take her hand to my crotch again and undo my pants and pull my pants down, so they are at my ankles. She starts jerking me off. I move her hand away.

I keep kissing her neck and I start to finger her again and take my dick and start rubbing the outside of her pussy with the tip of my dick. I reach into jacket to pull out a condom. The condom is attached to a second one, so too tough to tear open with teeth. I do not want to use my other hand to open the condom because I have had enough resistance so far. I do not want another state break...

I find a single condom also in my pocket. I pull it out. I tear it open with my teeth and unroll it on my dick. I slowly pull out my fingers, and I keep rubbing my dick up and down her slit. I have her hold my dick, and she helps me guide it inside of her.

Fucking on the couch is odd to me when I realize that a guy can come in at any second and see what is going on. No one will care, but it is odd. The sex is short the first round.

After we fuck, she tells me about the whole complicated story. The guy she was talking to earlier in the night was a friend that she has fucked a few times. Her seeing him threw her off because she was not expecting to see him, and things got weird after because he wanted more than just a hook up situation. On top of that, her boyfriend of 7 years is moving from New York to Vegas to live with her in three days. Candis says she and him have a love-hate relationship, and she is unsure if she actually wants him living in Vegas with her, but he said he will not keep a long distance relationship going anymore. She says she likes me and that everything happening tonight is probably a sign that she should not be with her boyfriend, but she has to see how things will play out. Candis says she wants to see me again but needs to give her New York boyfriend a chance since she has put so much time into the relationship.

It is 6:45am. Candis has a 30 minute drive to get home and a 30 minute drive from her home to work. She quickly gets dressed. She says maybe we can see each other Friday afternoon because her boyfriend does not fly in until that night. I agree and say that sounds fun.

CONCLUSION

One Night Stands are fun. Any guy can become a One Night Stand master in a short amount of time. These stories are a great springboard to learning about how to quickly and easily get the girl. To discover more secrets and see a full demonstration of how easy it is to get the girl, go to <u>getthegirltonight.com/one-night-stands</u>.

www.ingramcontent.com/pod-product-compliance
Lightning Source LLC
Chambersburg PA
CBHW020511030426
42337CB00011B/337